ENDORSE

Jesus made a remarkable statement in Matthew 18. He told His disciples that unless they changed and became like little children, they would never enter the kingdom of heaven. Darrell is one who has taken these words to heart and has discovered how to live by pure faith, simple obedience, and child-like wonder. Because of this, he has entered into the realm of the kingdom of heaven. This book is an invitation for you to experience the same. Read these pages with humble expectation and be prepared to get activated in the supernatural!

PASTOR DAVID OH
ENCOUNTER L.A. CHURCH

Darrell Benton is a modern-day hero of the Christian faith. He gives all glory to God as he boldly walks out his conviction in the power of Jesus to heal and save today! We need more people like Darrell in our society, especially in Christian circles. Darrell has a heart to see God move through healing and to see people encounter the love and power of God in tangible ways. This book is a great snapshot of his incredible journey. It challenges us all to walk by faith and carry the supernatural power of God, expressed through physical healing. There is great insight and wisdom within these pages for those who are hungry to grow and experience a breakthrough in the realm of miracles.

REVEREND ZACHARY KINTNER
SHERMAN OAKS PRESBYTERIAN CHURCH

HEAL

THE

SICK

DARRELL BENTON

Cover and Book Layout Design by Westerly Creative Studio.

Edited by Linda Benton, Linet Badali and Mark Miller.

For Worldwide Distribution. Printed in the United States of America.

ISBN: 978-0-578-48295-8

I dedicate this book to our Lord and Savior Jesus Christ. If not for the Holy Spirit leading me, this book would not have happened. Also to my mom Rose who has inspired me my entire life with her Christ-like unselfish love for everyone. And to my beautiful wife Linda who led me to the Lord in 2005 and has been so supportive in the writing of this book and did an amazing job editing it.

CONTENTS

FOREWORD

From the moment we encounter God, a personal transformation begins to take place where everyday moments can become incredible God stories. Whether you're behind a pulpit, out shopping, or at your workplace, you're going to be inspired that you, too, can make a difference and see God do great things. I think of the Scripture in Daniel where those who know their God will be strong and do exploits. Darrell had been a part of our HRock Church family since 2011 and serves faithfully on our ministry team. Darrell is one of those people who knows God, and as a result has seen and done exploits in the name of Jesus.

In Darrell Benton's new book Heal The Sick, he outlines keys to serving God with power and effectiveness. You'll read how God reached Darrell as a hitchhiking-hippie and anointed him in business and ministry, specifically in the area of faith for miracles. Through heartfelt stories, Darrell reveals practical steps to make everyday moments incredible God stories by stepping out in obedience. His unique and inspiring personal testimonies of healing and miracles will encourage you to believe and obey God and witness Him meet you in amazing ways. You, too, will experience the goodness of God and see Him do amazing things in and through you!

As you read Darrell's story of personal transformation, you'll find yourself relating to his steps of faith and obedience and be in awe of the amazing God we serve. God showed himself faithful to Darrell in his journey of faith, and I am confident He will do the same for you. When I think about Darrell's story, I think of the apostle Peter, a natural leader who was not afraid to step out in bold faith for Christ. Like Peter, Darrell has lived his life by faith, not afraid to step out of the boat and follow Jesus on the waters of life. Darrell's story will help you overcome fear and become a courageous follower of Christ. Darrell's story proves that God really does use all things for our good and His glory. From all sides of life — successes, failures, hardships, doubt, and redemption — see how God can weave all the different experiences of our lives into a beautiful tapestry of His grace and mercy. You'll find yourself laughing, crying, and inspired as you relate to this man of faith's story. Be encouraged as you read this book and let your faith grow in Christ for the miraculous!

CHÉ AHN
PRESIDENT OF HARVEST INTERNATIONAL MINISTRY
SENIOR PASTOR OF HROCK CHURCH
INTERNATIONAL CHANCELLOR OF WAGNER UNIVERSITY

1
—
HOW IT ALL STARTED FOR ME!

I grew up in a small town called Mount Vernon, tucked away in the southern part of Indiana. When I say "small," I mean it still does not have a Starbucks or department store in town. I had great parents, and my mom (who still resides there), well, she's the sweetest person in the world — somewhat comparable to Mother Theresa, and everyone in town knows and loves her. Currently, at the age of 90, she still volunteers at the Salvation Army soup kitchen feeding the needy. While growing up I only attended church a few times in my youth and wasn't sure if there really was a God.

One fateful day in 1975, when I was 22 years old, I ran into three guys that I knew. They asked me if I wanted to hitchhike to California with them. I thought about it for a whole five minutes and then blurted out, "Yeah, I'll go." So I went home and told my parents, and after they got over the shock, they each gave me $20 and wished me well. That very day, a crucial crossroad in my life, I took off hitchhiking with $40 in my pocket. There began my journey — the journey that would change my life forever.

We started our trip by splitting up into two pairs, thinking that we would get rides easier that way. When we got to Illinois, about 20 miles from home, as we continued to thumb for a ride, we saw a pickup truck slowing down as it approached us. Excited, thinking that we were going to get a ride, we were all smiles. The smiles were quickly wiped off our faces as the guys in the pickup truck threw beer cans at us, calling us "hippies" as they drove by without stopping. Right about then, my 19-year-old friend Don was starting to get a little nervous about the trip. I was a little shaken myself by that incident, but I shrugged it off as I did most things back then, when I didn't have a care in the world. That night, Don and I slept in a construction zone in East St. Louis. Don kept waking up throughout the night, thinking that he heard noises, but in the morning we woke up unharmed and continued on our journey. When we got to the shoulder on the highway, we saw another hitchhiker about 100 yards ahead of us. He got a ride first, and as their car passed by us, he smiled and tossed us a friendly joint. It might not be such a big deal today since marijuana is legal in a lot of places, but it was back then.

After some time, we scored ourselves a very welcomed ride from an individual who was headed to Oklahoma. Once there, we took shelter from the rain under a viaduct, waiting for our next ride. Eventually a lady, about 55 years old, picked us up. This I thought was strange considering she was by herself picking up a couple of longhaired hippies. She was very friendly and had a sweet charisma about her. Soon she began talking to us about God. Now, at that time in my life, I did not want to hear about God — in fact, I was agnostic and mostly into sex, drugs, and rock 'n' roll. Still, she was an intriguing lady, and to my surprise, I started enjoying listening to her.

Aside from the fact that I enjoyed talking with her, I actually felt a connection to her. Then she really got my attention when she started telling me that I was going to make a lot of money in my life and that I was going to help a lot of people. She spoke boldly and confidently, saying that she knew these things because she was very close to God. After a couple of hours of driving and talking, she said that she had to get off at the next exit.

When she pulled over at the side of the off-ramp to let us off, I noticed Don looked a little distressed. It seemed all this "God talk" made him a bit uneasy. As we were getting our backpacks out of the trunk, the lady reminded me again of the God-given message to me — that I was going to make a lot of money and help a lot of people — and she said a prayer for us. As we said our farewells, I told her we were going to walk over to the next on-ramp because it's easier to get rides when people are entering the freeway. But she said, "No, you won't have to walk over there, you'll get a ride right away, and you'll get a good job in California."

Without giving much thought to what she said, we were going to walk towards the on-ramp of Interstate 10 anyways. Sarcastically amused at what the lady had said to me, I was chuckling, but when I looked over at Don, he had a look of dead seriousness on his face. He was so bothered by my lack of seriousness that he started having heart palpitations. He wouldn't drop the matter and went on to express the importance of my taking her seriously. To help ease his mind, I replied with an "OK." Yet I had to have the last word. So, to prove a point as we walked to the side of the freeway instead of the next on-ramp, I stuck out my thumb and said, "If there's a God, then the very next car will stop."

To my utter astonishment, the driver of the very next car slammed on his brakes and came to a screeching halt. Inside sat a longhaired hippie that opened the back door for us with a stick. Still stunned with disbelief that my "testing God" worked, we jumped in the car. Then the driver stunned us some more with his story about him being a drug dealer from Norfolk, Virginia. A few days ago he had just come home from work and found narcotic agents at his apartment, so he decided to take off to California. We asked him where in California he was headed to, and he replied, "Orange County" — the exact same place we were going. The entire trip only took us three days from start to finish, about the same amount of time it would have taken us had we driven ourselves to California.

Within weeks of meeting that woman of God on our trip who had spoken prophetically over me, I found a job just like she had said I would, making $4 an hour in Los Angeles County. Now, considering that it was 1975, naively I thought that that salary was a lot of money. Little did I know just how much money I'd be making later on in my life. The road to my riches did involve some illicit activity such as drug dealing still in my hippie days, but I went on to make my real fortune legitimately owning a reputable company in the photo supply industry — another prophecy of hers that came true. I became a millionaire as my company grew to be the largest photographic supply distributor across America for Fuji and Mitsubishi. I just wish she'd have told me to go digital as soon as it was invented. I eventually lost my business and all of my assets with the rise of digital technology. As for the "helping a lot of people" part of her prophecy, I believe she was speaking to the fact that after accepting Jesus Christ as my personal Savior in 2005, I became involved in jail ministry as well as other ministries. Then in 2013, I began a life of helping fellow Christians release the power of the Holy Spirit into their lives and the lives of others around them. All in all, my life journey has been pretty incredible. My only regret was coming to accept Jesus Christ so late in my life at the age of 51. But now I realize that all those years that I felt were wasted, God actually used to serve His kingdom more powerfully, and I believe that this book is part of that lady's prophecy living on.

The power that raised Jesus Christ from the dead is revealed in Ephesians 1:19-20: "*And what is the exceeding greatness of his power to us-ward who believe, according to the working of his mighty power, which he wrought in Christ, when he raised him from the dead, and set him at his own right hand in the heavenly places.*" We all have that same power in us.

On another fateful day, January 2, 2005, my now wife, Linda, and I went on our first date, having first connected weeks before on a dating website. I knew she was a Christian, but it didn't scare me; and she knew I wasn't, and it didn't scare her. For Valentine's Day she bought me a Bible — my very first Bible with my name engraved in gold foil and all. Linda later says that that Bible was a fleece that she set before me. Well, I passed with flying colors. To my and Linda's surprise, as I started to read I was so captivated by the Word of God that I read the entire New Testament in just six weeks. Then I started reading Christian books written by famous authors. I was just soaking it all in like a sponge. Then one night, I had a dream that I was on an airplane that was crashing and Jesus saved me. That act of being saved by Christ created complete peace in my body. It had been some 40 years since the day I met that prophetic lady while hitchhiking, who now I believe to be an angel of God. Well, you know what they say: "better late than never." Thankfully, once I received salvation, my walk with Jesus took off pretty much at warp speed. I guess I was making up for lost time!

In late fall of 2005, Linda and I left the hustle and bustle of Los Angeles County and moved up to Nevada City in northern

California, and lived in the beautiful mountains of Sierra Nevada on a sprawling, picturesque, secluded property. It felt like we were honeymooning in paradise. The local church that we were attending was your typical nondenominational church that did not believe in the move of the Holy Spirit. In fact, they sadly discouraged it.

2

—

HELLO, SUPERNATURAL WORLD OF GOD

You, too, will also walk in this if you only believe!

It was three years after falling madly in love with Jesus that I got to experience firsthand the supernatural healing power of God in 2008. My right shoulder had been diagnosed with frozen shoulder, and I was looking for a surgeon to relieve me of the excruciating stabbing pain that I felt every time I tried raising my arm. It felt as though someone was stabbing me with an ice pick.

Through a local Christian men's breakfast club I met a sweet man named Dieter, who became a dear friend of mine. Dieter attended a different church and introduced me to a fascinating couple. In conversation this couple told me about a healing room at Bethel Church in Redding, California. This was something I had never heard of before, and I became extremely curious and wanted to learn more. Redding was only about three hours north of Nevada City, where we were living at the time. They told me that people from all over the world traveled to this healing room — hurt, injured, diseased, or ill — but walked out miraculously healed and made whole again.

Now, I know what you're thinking: "How could this be?" Well, I had a revelation, and I have to say that it actually made complete sense to me. You see, I realized that if you really believed in God, then how could you possibly doubt the fact that He is capable of doing anything and everything? We worship a God who spoke the world into creation. He made man from dust and — just as quickly — breathed life into him. If we can believe that we have eternal life through Jesus, then why wouldn't we think that He could do a simple thing like heal someone, especially since diseases don't exist in God's kingdom?

This kind of thinking takes what I would like to call "simple-minded" thinking. I am not referring to "simple-minded" thinking as in "stupid" or "naïve," but rather as in thoughts that are simple and not overly complicated. In other words, the type of thought that takes things for their face value. We only have to believe that God can heal and that He wants to do it for everyone. (I will go into more detail later in the book about that.)

I have seen hundreds of healing miracles in the last six years. And you can, too, if you don't complicate it and just believe what the Word of God says. John 14:12 says, "*Verily, verily, I say unto you, He that believeth on me, the works that I do shall he do also; and greater works than these shall he do; because I go unto my Father.*" If you are going to read the Bible, then I invite you to take it for its full face value and actually believe it.

OK, back to my story: To be absolutely sure that going to Bethel Church was something that God wanted me to do, I got down on my knees in prayer. This was probably the first time in my life that I distinctly heard from God, and I knew He wanted me to go to Bethel for healing. I called my friend Dieter to share this with him, and he responded, "That's great, but there is also a local church that walks in the gift of healing. Why don't you try them out first?" I figured it couldn't hurt, so Dieter and I went together, and I had three people pray over me there. I am not sure if I didn't receive the healing that day because of my lack of faith, or if it was due to their lack of confidence, or perhaps it was both. Either way, I was sure that God wanted me to go to Bethel Church, and with that, I drove up there a few weeks later.

After making the three-hour drive to Redding on a Saturday morning, I arrived at the church and signed in. In the lobby I met a few people who had traveled there from other countries. This gave me tremendous confidence for healing because I thought, "Why would these people be coming from all over the world to be healed if it didn't work?" After some time had passed, I was ushered into a waiting room where there was worship music playing and other people waiting to go into the actual healing room. I was a little disappointed when I found out it was another waiting room. I was so spiritually and physically ready to re-ceive my healing, I just wanted to cut to the chase — this wasn't moving fast enough for me. As I was forced to wait, I noticed some young adults were going around the room, waving flags to worship music. At first I thought it was weird, but then I started to enjoy it and found myself basking in this Spirit-filled atmo-sphere. While we were basking, I could hear announcements of individuals that got healed. One of those individuals was a man who just had his deaf ears opened. My impatience completely gone now, I was thoroughly enjoying myself, basking and soak-ing in His glory — in fact, I could have stayed there all day.

When they did finally call my name, I immediately jumped up and proceeded into the healing room. I sat down in a row of chairs, awaiting further instructions while watching a guy joyful-ly blowing on a shofar. Shortly afterward, a young man and mid-dle-aged woman approached me and asked what was going on with me, so I told them about my shoulder. They started praying for me, and incredibly after a few minutes, I was able to raise my arm all the way up! This was the very same arm that shot excruciating, stabbing pain every time I tried raising it. Miraculously, about 95% of the pain was gone. WOW — YAY GOD!

Reeling from my healing, on the drive home I tested my healing and put my right arm out to the side in front of the passenger seat, which would have triggered pain — but lo and behold, no pain! Then I put my arm behind the passenger seat, and piercing pain shot up my arm. I was crushed. I heard Satan say to me (not in an audible voice), "Darrell, you stupid idiot! You didn't get healed." However, I immediately remembered what they told me at Bethel: that Satan would try to steal the healing and that I was to command it to leave in Jesus' name. That's precisely what I did, and the pain went away. Praise and glory to God that it has never come back, to this day!

This was a pivotal turning point in my life. I was never the same after this experience. That is why I am so passionate about the healing ministry. This supernatural healing that I experienced is what brought Jesus to life for me. It made Him real. My faith soared, and all of the doubts that I had started to dissipate. Why does Matthew 14:7 state that few find the narrow gate to salvation? I think that it's because many don't really believe in their heart that Jesus is the Savior. It is OK to admit that you have doubts and unbelief; God sees your heart and knows exactly what you are thinking. Just ask Him for help. Mark 9:24 says, "*And straightway the father of the child cried out, and said with tears, Lord, I believe; help thou mine unbelief.*" I remember that I used to have doubts during the first three years as a Christian because I couldn't wrap my mind around eternity. How could it be possible to live forever? It just didn't make sense. The more I would think about it, the more I would doubt it. After my healing experience, Jesus became very real to me. I quit trying to figure out how eternity and the supernatural worked and just accepted it.

Fast forward to today: I see miracles on a regular basis. Glory to God, they have become a weekly occurrence for me. If I don't release the power that is in me (see Ephesians 3:20) and all born-again Christians, I am taking away the glory of God. I would never want to do that. A few days ago, I was volunteering at a healing miracle conference with my grandson Shane. We were praying for a girl about 15 years old that had been in an accident. Her right foot was angled out to the side, and she couldn't walk normally. After we commanded it to straighten out in the name of Jesus, she started to weep uncontrollably. Her foot straightened out, and she was able to walk normally again.

One Sunday at HRock Church in Pasadena, California (where Linda and I currently attend and have been members since 2013), I noticed two women walking into the sanctuary at the same time. One of them walking was with a crutch and with significant pain in her left hip. Her friend asked me if I could help them find an aisle seat for them since her friend couldn't maneuver very well. I responded, "Well, let's just fix the problem," so I asked her to come out into the lobby. (Note: Once you start walking in healing, you don't even think about it; you just know they will be healed.) I told her that all of her pain was going to go away because this was easy for Jesus. I received a word of knowledge that her left leg was shorter than her right. We found a nearby chair, and she sat down. I commanded her left leg to grow out evenly with the right leg, and it immediately shot out — becoming even with the right. She started crying and said that her pain was gone! I love it when people cry after experiencing Jesus. It excites me to know that their life will never be the same. The lady picked up her crutch and carried it back into the sanctuary.

I was recently rear-ended on the freeway, and my car was totaled. It was a multiple-car collision, and the next day I called the lady that was driving the car that my car was hurled into and asked her how she was doing. She said that there was discomfort in her arm. Without a second thought, I prayed for her, speaking to the problem. Thanks be to the power and glory of God, she responded with "Wow! It all went away!"

The next day I went to the body shop that was putting together the estimate for my car. After taking care of business with the lady behind the counter, I started sharing Jesus with her. As I was sharing, another female employee walked in and sat down next to her. I could literally sense Jesus in this woman, so I told her that very thing. She responded by saying that she needed to hear that, so I said that that was why I said it. I transitioned into telling her about the healing miracles that I see and told her about how certain back problems can be caused by having one leg shorter than the other. With this, she immediately admitted to having pain in her back and agreed to let me have a look at her legs. I noticed that her left leg was about half an inch shorter than her right leg. Now, normally I would command the leg to grow out evenly with the other leg before anything would happen. However, this time as soon as I started to speak the words "I command," the leg shot out! A look of shock came across her face. I asked her if she felt it grow out, and she blurted out that she felt something. I then asked her to stand up to test whether or not her pain was gone. She stood up and with excitement in her voice exclaimed, "Yes, the pain went away!" She walked back behind the counter, where her co-worker was, and they both started staring at me most peculiarly as if saying, "Who are you?" I looked at them and said, "It's Jesus. He loves you." A week later I returned to the body shop to check on the status of my car. That same lady was there again standing behind the counter. She jubilantly told me the pain never returned. Glory to God!

A few days after that, I was on the phone with a lady in Kansas from the car insurance company, and I got a word of knowledge about her lower back pain. When I asked her about it, she confirmed that she did have this pain. After I spoke to the pain, commanding it to go away in Jesus' name, she said that it definitely felt different. Generally speaking, miracles on a daily basis have become a normal, routine way of life for me, and they can be for you, too. That is what this book is about. I am going to explain everything in simple, down-to-earth, layman's terms. The more of us are out there walking in these miracles, the more lives are touched and transformed as we bring a living Jesus to a dying world.

We are so fortunate to live in the times that we are living in. In Luke 10:24, Jesus said, "*For I tell you, that many prophets and kings have desired to see those things which ye see, and have not seen them; and to hear those things which ye hear, and have not heard them.*" Once you learn how to release God's power and to be more Spirit-led, this verse will make more sense to you. Many in the Body of Christ are praying and waiting for revival, and that's all good and well, and I do believe in praying and hoping for all good things. Nevertheless, I also believe in what He has already done and believe in our God-given authority to physically release His power. When we do this, we bring revival into being.

God poured out His Spirit some 2,000 years ago into the spiritual realm, and it is always available to those that believe it. It is time for us to do what Jesus commanded us to do in Matthew 28:19-20. He said, "*Go ye therefore, and teach all nations, baptizing them in the name of the Father, and of the Son, and of the Holy Ghost: Teaching them to observe all things whatsoever I have commanded you: and, lo, I am with you always, even unto the end of the world."* **Notice how He said,** *"Teaching them to observe all things whatsoever I have commanded you."* **This scripture is known as the Great Commission that is for all of us, not just the apostles. He has commanded us in Matthew 10:8 to** *"Heal the sick, cleanse the lepers, raise the dead, cast out devils: freely ye have received, freely give."* **Jesus ascended into heaven and handed us the baton to release His power to all those who choose to receive it, and He wants us to have fun while doing this. You are going to love doing this, and it will, in turn, inspire others around you.**

In Matthew 11:11, Jesus said, *"Verily I say unto you, Among them that are born of women there hath not risen a greater than John the Baptist: notwithstanding he that is least in the kingdom of heaven is greater than he."* **It wasn't until I came to the revelation of exactly who I was in Christ that I comprehended this. I believe all born-again Christians ought to read the Bible and desire the same level of anointing and impact that the biblical mighty men of God had. Among them are Abraham, Moses, Joshua, David, and Paul, just to name a few. Every born-again Christian carries the kingdom of heaven within them — solely because Jesus resides in them and Jesus is the kingdom of heaven. (I may have lost some of you here, but keep reading and I will attempt to win you over to this truth.) God said that my people are destroyed for lack of knowledge (Hosea 4:6). This book will help you come to know your true identity in Christ and help you progress in your newfound knowledge of God's promises and truths.**

In the Old Testament, the Holy Spirit was not given to everyone. It was only given to certain people and for a specific period of time. In Numbers 11:17, when Moses was overwhelmed to

the brink of exhaustion dealing with all the disagreements and complaining of the Israelites, God told him, "*And I will come down and talk with thee there: and I will take of the spirit which is upon thee, and will put it upon them; and they shall bear the burden of the people with thee, that thou bear it not thyself alone.*" **Moses picked out 70 people to help him, and God knew that they would need the Holy Spirit to take on the task.**

Saul first received the Holy Spirit in 1 Samuel 10:10 and prophesied among people. Later, in chapter 16 verse 14, Saul lost the Holy Spirit and received a spirit that tormented him. Saul was under a different covenant than the one we are under today. As the author of Hebrews points out in Hebrews 8:6, "*But now hath he obtained a more excellent ministry, by how much also he is the mediator of a better covenant, which was established upon better promises.*" Everything changed after Jesus gave His life on the cross. The grace we now have, along with the new spirit and new heart, empowers us to walk as Jesus did in this world. The Holy Spirit dwells in us (John 14:17). When you come to fully understand this and start to witness His power flowing through you, it will manifest peace in your life, and you will enjoy all the fruits of the Spirit (Galatians 5:22). Thus making ministry effortless and miracles the new norm.

At church we are cautiously told not to do too much (e.g., serving on the prayer ministry team every week because it'll burn us out). However, there is no "burn out" for me because it is merely about "being" instead of actually "doing." This is who we are in Christ. Healing just happens, like breathing just hap-pens. What we do at church on the ministry team is no different than what we do anywhere else. In other words, it's not like you should be "trying" to heal somebody, but rather realize that you are simply a vessel to "release" His power to manifest the provi-sions that He already died for. It's all about the finished work of the cross.

Let's take it one step further. The baptism of the Holy Spirit is available today. It has changed my life and has changed many of my friends' lives as well. Receiving the Baptism of the Holy Spirit is extremely important in order to walk into your destiny as a "Spirit-filled" Christian. Some churches don't believe that this is available for us today, but I assure you that it is. I pray in tongues often to build myself up in my faith (Jude 1:20), along with many other benefits that come with it. After I received the baptism of the Holy Spirit, there was a definite change in my life and my walk with Jesus.

Jesus was baptized by the Holy Spirit in Matthew 3:16. Upon being baptized, Jesus rose up from the water. The Bible says that the heavens were opened to Him and He saw the Spirit of God descending like a dove alighting upon Him. He didn't walk in any miracles until He received this baptism. In Acts 10:38 we learn that Jesus of Nazareth was anointed by God with the Holy Spirit and with power. He went about doing good and healing all who were oppressed by the devil, for God was with Him. This was the reason why Jesus told His disciples in Acts 1:4 to wait in Jerusalem until they received the baptism of the Holy Spirit and that once it had come upon them, they would be filled with power (Acts 1:8).

Being baptized by the Holy Spirit also changed Peter in great ways. Before this, he famously denied Jesus three times before the rooster crowed. His change was evident in Acts 3. The Bible tells of a man who was lame from birth; this man was carried to the temple every day to receive alms from those entering. When Peter and John walked up to the temple, Peter told him, "*Silver and gold have I none; but such as I have give I thee: In the name of Jesus Christ of Nazareth rise up and walk*" (Acts 3:6). This man immediately stood up and went about leaping and praising God in the temple. Notice the part where Peter said, "*but such as I have give I thee.*" By asking and believing, Peter received the power of the Holy Spirit, and we can, too. To receive the baptism of the Holy Spirit, simply ask for it with belief.

Jesus also thought it was essential for us to receive water baptism. That's why it's written in the Bible. Every word in the Bible is real, and when we genuinely believe what we read in our hearts and minds, we will begin to walk out in His power. A Bible study leader once jokingly said of me, "Darrell here believes every word in the Bible, and it's inspiring." All I can say in response is that it's all about believing. As far as I'm concerned, if it's in the Bible — the living Word of God — it's true.

3

—

VISION

See yourself walking in the power of Jesus!

Seven years ago, when I first started pouring over as many books on the supernatural as I could get ahold of, I was amazed at the number of miracles that were still going on today. As I continued to learn about the wonders that Jesus and His disciples did in the Bible, my faith became further grounded. This confirmed everything that I had come to believe and created a lot of excitement in me. Somehow I realized that I had completely overlooked the act of pure belief in Scriptures such as John 14:12: *"Verily, verily, I say unto you, He that believeth on me, the works that I do shall he do also; and greater works than these shall he do; because I go unto my Father."*

Leafing through some old notes that I had jotted down while reading the Bible about nine years ago, I came upon that very Scripture. Why didn't I believe this Scripture at the time? Well, two reasons. The first one was that my pastor at the time and his congregation didn't believe that healings exist today. And secondly, I had no knowledge of just who I was in Christ Jesus nine years ago. This revelation is so crucial to living a healthy, full, empowered Christian life. It saddens me to see so many

Christians living powerless, mediocre lives because so many churches fail to teach us this life-altering, wonderful reality.

When Jesus ascended to heaven, He handed us the responsibility to do greater works than He did, works that will result in kingdom advancement. I don't ever want to let Jesus down because of false humility or for any other reason that my carnal mind might tell me. Especially knowing that the enemy will be telling us lies to hold us back from doing kingdom work that Jesus commanded us to do.

Many years ago I attended a business seminar. The one phrase that stuck in my mind was "Successful people don't make excuses. Successful people make money." Let's take this phrase and apply it to Christians. I believe that successful Christians don't make excuses. They release God's love and power to the world the way we were commanded to do. Naturally, we were all created different and therefore process our thoughts differently. It is vitally important that you have a vision of yourself being used by God for the healing of others. He loves us all equally and shows no partiality. Throughout the Bible, He has used many imperfect people to carry out His plans. When we submit to His will, His plans become our plans because we are transformed into living sacrifices for Him, and His power manifests itself in our everyday lives. You will learn how to do this later on in this book.

Moses committed murder, Jacob deceived his dad, Isaac, and stole his brother's inheritance, and David murdered and committed adultery. Even if you have done worse than this, God can still use you because you are made righteous through the blood of Jesus. The enemy will try to convince you that you are not worthy of the thoughts that the Holy Spirit embedded in your mind. However, you need to understand that although God is giving you a revelation of the great things He wants you to accomplish, you must first believe what the living Word of God says about all of us. Once you do this, you should then shun the lies that the enemy is trying to convince you of and all the lies that pessimistic and insecure people might try to convince you of. Ask the Holy Spirit for help in believing that you can partici- pate in sharing His power, His love, and His grace with others.

A while back, I was going through the checkout line at a grocery store, and I asked the cashier how she was doing be- cause she looked a little tired. She said that her feet were sore because she had been standing all day. There was a line behind me, so I quickly told her that I could make that pain go away. She replied with an "OK." I then commanded in the name of Je- sus Christ for her pain to go away and thanked Him for this heal- ing. She had a big smile on her face and reported that the pain was almost all gone. If I had cared about what everyone in the line thought about me, I wouldn't have stepped out to heal her. My "non-action" would then have prevented God's glory from manifesting, and she would have depended on over-the-counter pain-relieving drugs instead of experiencing God's healing pow- er. That lady, along with all the people standing in line, would have never experienced or seen God's glory. At the beginning of my walk in this healing ministry, I didn't wholly believe that this was for me. When I first started pursuing God's power in my life, I would ask the Holy Spirit for His wisdom and for His will on a daily basis. Believe me when I say that He wants His power to flow through you, to heal the ones that He loves. Jesus asked Peter to feed His "sheep," and He wants you to do the same.

In 1952 Florence Chadwick attempted to swim from the California coast to Catalina Island 22 miles away. Small boats accompanied her to keep an eye out for sharks and to assist her in case she grew too weary to go on. About 15 hours into the swim, thick fog was setting in and so was her exhaustion. An hour later, succumbing to her exhaustion, she asked to be pulled out. Climbing into the boat, now able to see the coastline, she discovered that she had stopped just one mile short of her destination. You can just imagine how crushed she must have felt. But rather than drowning in her sorrows, lamenting on her failure to achieve her goal, two months later she tried again. This time, she kept a mental image of the shoreline in her mind. This helped her make it all the way! My suggestion to you is to believe what the Word of God says you can do. Like Florence Chadwick, don't let fog or fatigue deter your goal. Visualize yourself as a co-laborer of Jesus Christ. Jesus said He is the vine and we are the branches and that we can do nothing without Him. Since you aren't without Him, know that you can do all things. If you believe Philippians 4:13, that you can do all things through Christ, it will happen for you. When we believe, we receive, but when we doubt, we do without. It has worked for me, and I know without a shadow of doubt in my mind that it will work for you, too — so just believe.

Memorizing Scriptures is a great way to get started in this ministry. Your vision becomes clear when these Scriptures become part of you, but you must believe them in your heart. God thought it was important for Joshua to meditate on His Word day and night to become prosperous. Joshua 1:8 says, "*This book of the law shall not depart out of thy mouth; but thou shalt meditate therein day and night, that thou mayest observe to do according to all that is written therein: for then thou shalt make thy way prosperous, and then thou shalt have good success.*"

You can't meditate on His Word if you don't know it. I am surprised at the number of people who want to walk in this healing anointing, yet don't have some of these Scriptures — let alone any — memorized. A few Scriptures that I recommend to memorize are John 14:12, Mark 16:16,18, Isaiah 53:5, 1 Peter

2:24, and Matthew 8:17. As you read the Bible, choose verses that speak to you, and memorize and meditate on them. Affirmations are another good way of having your dreams and desires become a reality. As part of your affirmation, you can recite things such as "I have become the righteousness of God in Him; I have received Christ Jesus the Lord, so I walk in Him; I have the mind of Christ." Find the Scriptures that work for you. Read them in the morning and before going to bed until they become a reality in your life.

4
—
SURRENDER

Surrender is not optional; you must do it!

To surrender simply means to give up control or possession of. I believe that we all have a desire to control others or to control certain situations that we find ourselves in. Regardless of the degree of control that you may personally want in these areas, it is imperative that you learn to surrender to God's will in your life first, before you can obtain a close relationship with Him. God is not looking for golden or silver vessels, only for ones that are surrendered.

If you were to ask most Christians whether or not they have surrendered to God, they would probably answer that they have. Nobody wants to be thought of as a bad Christian or someone that is not following the rules. Genuinely surrendering to God is probably the hardest thing for our carnal mind to do. From an early age, we have been programmed to think of ourselves as the reason we succeed or fail in life. This is true for the physical world that we live in. However, it is completely different in the spiritual world, where our success or failure is no longer dependent on ourselves but is rather reliant on our faith in what the Bible says we can do through Christ.

Those who have had positive reinforcement in their lives from sources such as parents, teachers, coaches, television, etc., will undoubtedly have a better chance of success in life. The problem is that success in this world is not the same as success in the spiritual world. Those of you who were raised by parents who taught you that you can do all things through Christ, who strengthens you, will have a much more balanced and rewarding life. This revelation is the key to achieving real success in this world and in the kingdom.

On the other end of the spectrum, some of you grew up brainwashed with malicious lies coming from either your parents or others around you. You grew up with low self-esteem, thinking that you are not worthy of accomplishing anything of significance. And as a result, you let your failures reinforce that false assumption. And then when something does go right, you're more apt to attribute it to mere luck or coincidence.

The state of our minds today has been shaped over the years by the negative or positive influences in our lives. Sometimes even positive reinforcement can deter us. When we have a very positive opinion of ourself, we feel confident enough to achieve our goals in life and overcome most of the obstacles we run into. Scenarios like this can make it challenging to surrender our independent, self-reliant way of thinking because we have become so programmed to depend on ourselves, making it difficult to depend on God. To those of you who have had more negative influences, you may feel unworthy to receive help from the Holy Spirit. Feeling "unworthy" means not knowing who you are in Christ (which is something we'll delve into deeper later in this book).

When I first became a Christian 14 years ago, I learned something valuable. A pastor that I used to watch on television taught me to get on my knees when I prayed. Getting into this physical stance during prayer somehow made me realize how big He is and how small I am. Later on I learned how much He loves me and how much He wants to use me in releasing His power to the broken world that we live in. There was an absolute peace that came over me once I had this understanding. The revelation, that God is a huge God and is a Father to me personally, came from this experience. It was in that moment that I first felt a personal connection with my Lord and Savior, Jesus Christ. This relationship has indeed grown into something much bigger and more fruitful for me since then, and you are on that journey as well!

Learning to surrender to Jesus will begin to remove our desires for acceptance from our peers, and rather wanting approval from Jesus Himself. In Matthew 10:38-39, Jesus said, *"And he that taketh not his cross, and followeth after me, is not worthy of me. He that findeth his life shall lose it: and he that loseth his life for my sake shall find it."* Some may find Matthew 10:35 a bit harsh when Jesus said that he came to set "man" against his own family. Jesus knew that not all would accept Him, including some of our family members. Christianity is not a casual way of life where you go to church once or twice a week or volunteer somewhere so you can feel good and have acceptance from others. Losing our lives for Jesus' sake means that you are "all in" and that you have decided to let every thought become captive to the obedience of Jesus Christ. What this means for you and me is that everything we do in our daily lives we should do as if we were doing it unto the Lord. Satan always gets fence-sitters, or those not fully sold on Jesus. There is a common saying in churches that says, "God is first, family second, ministry third, and then everything else." I believe that God is first and there is no second.

When I put God first, I am able to love my family and everyone else much more. His love flows through me and to the world around me — instead of my human love, which is selfish. We need to learn how to be Spirit-led; I will discuss this further in an upcoming chapter. If all of this sounds hard to believe, I urge you to give it a try. You will experience the same benefits as I have and will be able to live life as God intended. Peace, love, and joy come from a life of surrender. You really do gain your life when you lose it.

God revealed to me that the most significant stumbling block to walking in the supernatural is a failure to surrender to Him. When we ultimately give everything over to God, we gain our life and begin to walk in His power. God can't get the best of us until our human will is dissolved. Many of the miracles that I have seen have been the result of emptying me of my carnal thoughts, surrendering to the Holy Spirit, and allowing the Holy Spirit to guide my words. Many times when I'm praying for the sick, I will command healing in a certain part of their body that they haven't even told me about. Not only will this usually surprise them, but it will also get them to acknowledge the fact that they didn't even tell me about that pain or illness. With a smile, I will usually respond by saying, "Yes, I know, but Jesus told me because He loves you and doesn't want you to have that pain."

Surrender is simply allowing Jesus to lead you in all areas of your life, and putting little value on your needs and great value on His. Delight yourself in Him and He will give you the desires of your heart. My most favorite thing to do now is to minister to others.

5

—

PRAYER

Simply communing with Jesus!

Prayer is a crucial part of Christian life. God created us so that we can have a special relationship with Him. When we set aside time for prayer, we are fulfilling His desire for a relationship with us. The more time we spend alone with Him, the closer our relationship with our Lord and Savior Jesus Christ becomes. The majority of the time we spend with Him should be spent listening to what He has to say to us rather than us telling Him what our desires are. Ask the Holy Spirit for help in hearing His voice; this will be a prayer that He will most definitely answer. Be patient and pray with the belief that you will receive. The Scriptures are clear about us doing this. James 1:6-8 says, *"But let him ask in faith, nothing wavering. For he that wavereth is like a wave of the sea driven with the wind and tossed. For let not that man think that he shall receive any thing of the Lord. A double minded man is unstable in all his ways."* Furthermore, Romans 12:3 states, *"according as God hath dealt to every man the measure of faith."* Believe what the Bible says: that you have this faith. Open your heart when you read the Bible, and accept that every word was written for you — because it was. God wants a relationship where you know that you can trust Him and believe that He loves you unconditionally and will for eternity. Without your complete trust in this, the connection you build with God cannot flourish. Don't concern yourself with trying to figure out whether or not all things are possible with God. Instead, believe that they are!

Personally, I thoroughly enjoy spending time with God in the mornings. Throughout the years, our relationship has advanced so much so that I experience His presence physically every day. For example, the moment I sit down to spend one-on-one time with Him, I begin to feel tingling electricity going through both of my hands. When it becomes more intense, I start to feel pressure on my palms. It feels as though the Holy Spirit is pushing onto my hands just so I'll know that He is there with me. Sometimes I can physically see an oil-like substance form on the tips of my fingers, and at its most intense level, it covers my entire hands. Usually, as I sit there asking God for His direction, I notice that if He agrees with the direction I believe He wants me to take, the electricity and pressure tend to increase. This isn't to say that all of you will hear from God in this manner.

God speaks to each of us in different ways. Find out how He communicates with you. It took me a while, and I don't claim to hear God's voice correctly all the time, but I am continually pursuing a closer bond with Him. It's imperative that you spend alone time with God for an intimate relationship with Him. Enter His gates with praise and thanksgiving, telling Him how much you love Him, and ask for His guidance in all things. Then watch your life, which seemed out of sorts, begin to come together when you learn to trust Him. Most of your time spent in God's presence should be spent listening to Him. This will result in His love, power, and grace flowing through you to others, and you will come to learn why Jesus said, "When you give up your life, you gain it."

The Scriptures confirm that God is a loving Father who wants to give us good gifts. Take a look at Matthew 7:9-11: "*Or what man is there of you, whom if his son ask bread, will he give him a stone? Or if he ask a fish, will he give him a serpent? If ye then, being evil, know how to give good gifts unto your children, how much more shall your Father which is in heaven give good things to them that ask him?*" As 2 Timothy 3:16 teaches us, the Bible was written by man but breathed and inspired by God.

The Scriptures show us that God has feelings just like we do. Examples of this are when the Bible speaks of God being a jealous God or Jesus showing anger when He turned over the money changers' tables in the temple. Now knowing this, how do you think it makes Him feel when He gives us these Scriptures, yet we still do not believe His Word? As our relationship develops with Him through prayer, our belief increases, and our prayers become more efficient. I can personally tell you that at the beginning of my journey into the healing ministry, I didn't have the faith that I have now. In my continued persistence and desire to please Him, spending more time delving into God's Word, my faith has grown substantially and will continue to do so.

God wants to give you good gifts, even more than you want to receive them. John 14:13-14 says, "*And whatsoever ye shall ask in my name, that will I do, that the Father may be glorified in the Son. If ye shall ask any thing in my name, I will do it.*" 1 Corinthians 12 speaks of nine different gifts of the Spirit, all of which are for the edification of the Body of Christ. Personally, I spent a lot of time praying for the gift of healing. I lacked the knowledge of praying expectantly in faith. It took about a year of praying and hoping until the gift finally manifested in my life. I was doing what Paul told us to do in 1 Corinthians 12:31: "*But covet earnestly the best gifts: and yet shew I unto you a more excellent way."* Evidently, Paul thought that having the gifts would show you a more excellent way to live by giving you another means to serve God. Keep in mind that He wouldn't have told us to desire them had they not been attainable.

A great example of this gift presented itself just yesterday, on Christmas Eve 2018. While at a restaurant, I asked a lady if she had back pain. Unfortunately, she replied with a short, curt "no." You must be OK with the fact that sometimes you'll get it wrong, or that people might think you are weird and therefore don't want to admit that they have a problem. This is especially true when you're out in public. Either way though, you need to understand that God is pleased with us when we do step out and contend for kingdom advancements. Embarrassment should not deter you from praying for healing over anybody. Not in the least bit downbeat, I left the restaurant with my friend Dan and went to a lady's home to pray for her. When she answered the door, she had a cane in her hand. It was apparent that she was having a difficult time walking and keeping herself steady on it. After explaining to her that God had already made provisions for her healing, I went on to quote some Scriptures to prove it. I then sat her down and, in Jesus' name, commanded her right leg to grow out even with her left leg, as Dan was praying over her feet and legs. In no time at all, she was able to get up out of her chair by herself and walk around without the cane! It was exciting to see her move her toes and bend over — almost touching the ground — when this wasn't something she was able to do just a few minutes before. God is so good that her healing didn't stop there. We also commanded her stage 4 cancer to leave her body in Jesus' name. I genuinely believe that it is now gone. She was thrilled and stunned at all that had happened.

Aside from the gift of healing, "word of knowledge" was another gift that I was in hot pursuit of and eventually received. The gift of healing blesses people once their pain or disease goes away. However, I believe that the gift of word of knowledge makes people feel singled out and special and blows them away because there is no way we could have known such intimate details about them. These can include, but are not limited to, the part of their body that the pain resides in, what their favorite toy was growing up, what their favorite color is, etc. These are little details that are revealed to us by God, the one who knows His sons and daughters so intimately that He knows the number of hairs on our head. Receiving a word of knowledge is personal, allowing for the receiver of the word to connect with God on a whole new level.

"Discernment of spirits" is also a valuable gift for the Church. Not only can I discern evil spirits that need to be cast out, but I can also discern Jesus in other Christians. Aside from my experiences yesterday with the lady at the restaurant and the older woman whom my friend Dan and I visited, I told another lady I saw at the grocery store that I could see Jesus in her. With a look of surprise, she asked, "You can?" I said, "Yes, and do you know how much He loves you?" She replied, "Yes I do." Sensing that she might have back pain, I asked her. She confirmed that she did. I prayed, commanding the pain in her back to go away in Jesus' name. After I was finished, I asked whether or not her back pain was gone. Amazed and excited, she exclaimed, "Yes, it feels different!" As I began telling her that Jesus didn't want her to have that pain, she paused, her eyes wandering into space, and said, "I've really felt like something has been missing in my life. I now realize what it is. I need to go back to church." Nodding in agreement, I replied, "That would definitely be a good idea. You need to let the love of Jesus flow through you, touching others, as it flows out of you." I can only imagine what a beautiful Christmas Jesus gave this woman. Not only had she heard from God, but she had also been healed of her back pain.

This is the typical Christian life that Jesus intends for us to live. All of you who believe will also walk in these miracles on a daily basis. I have heard people use Scriptures as an excuse for why they may not receive the "gifts." They often quote 1 Corinthians 12:11: "B*ut all these worketh that one and the self-same Spirit, dividing to every man severally as he wil*l." Individuals who constantly look at reasons for why things are not going to happen will not receive the good gifts of the Father. Instead, you should focus on the fact that Paul instructed us to desire the best gifts. Furthermore, believe that if we desire them with the correct heart, the Spirit will give them to us. A "correct" heart means that you are doing it to serve God, to serve others, and to help edify the Church. Please understand that spiritual gifts are not given to us for personal recognition or for your own self-advancement. I also want to add that it's not imperative to have the "gift of healing" in order to experience healing (Mark 16:17-18). All born-again believers have the power in them to release His power for healings and miracles. It doesn't matter what spiritual gifts you walk in; just strive to obtain the gifts. They are a lot of fun and produce tons of fruit.

Don't get discouraged if you are a person who tends to have negative thoughts about your life's circumstances. I used to be a very negative person. I remember a time when I was a distributor in the photographic industry, and one of the reps from a manufacturer went as far as saying that if he ever wanted to know anything negative about the industry, I would be the first person he would call. That comment said it all. It was practically common knowledge: I was a very negative person and had a negative outlook on certain things. However, now that I am a new creation in Christ, I have learned to renew my carnal mind and to have it draw into an agreement with the Spirit of God.

Private prayer produces public power. Matthew 6:6 says, *"But thou, when thou prayest, enter into thy closet, and when thou hast shut thy door, pray to thy Father which is in secret; and thy Father which seeth in secret shall reward thee openly."* Personally, I love it when He rewards me openly. Understand that the reward can come in many different shapes and sizes. Some examples can be the gifts of the Spirit, while others might be the fruit of our ministry. All in all, He will reward us in a way that we desire, as long as our desire is aligned with His.

Because of all the personal time I spend with God, my prayers produce public power, and as promised in His Word, I am also rewarded openly. A specific memory comes to mind of a time I prayed for a lady at church with stage 4 breast cancer. After praying for that woman's healing, not only did God remove the breast cancer, but He also removed the metal clip that had been placed in her breast during the biopsy. I love this! It's almost like God was showing off. This was God showing His power publicly, through me. As you can imagine, this miracle rewarded both the woman and me. To this day, I feel so happy when she greets me at church with a sunny smile and joyful hug. It is beautiful that we get to glorify God at church in so many ways. With our outstretched arms reaching toward the heavens while singing worship songs, we serve a God that sees our hearts and loves it when we give all praise, glory, and honor to Him. He is a God who will answer our sincere, faith-filled prayers. In the quiet places, our prayers invite the Holy Spirit to reveal to us the power that we have within us. You are a vessel of God that is waiting to explode with His power — to a world that desperately needs it.

6
—
OBEY GOD

*This is so easy when you have
surrendered to Him!*

Obeying God is actually a lot of fun if we have surrendered
to Him and genuinely want to please Him. It is so much easier
to focus on pleasing Him than being focused on pleasing ourselves. If you don't experience the fruits of the Spirit that are revealed in Galatians 5:22, it may be because you haven't learned
how to obey God. It's not like God is up in heaven with a big
stick, waiting to punish us if we don't obey Him. But do understand that all of His commandments are for our benefit and the
benefit of others.

Think of our relationship with God like the one an earthly
father would have with his child. Our kids don't always believe
that it is in their best interest to stay away from drugs, the
wrong crowds, etc. Yet because our experience and wisdom
discern what is best for them, although they don't always see
it, we try to guide them in the right direction. The same is true
for God, our heavenly Father. His knowledge far surpasses our
own understanding. We are His sheep and need to learn how
to discern His voice to follow His guidance. If you are having a

hard time hearing God's voice, a tip I'd like to share with you is merely to believe that you can hear Him. It sounds crazy simple, but it works. It is like the time I started presuming that people would be healed, and then it actually started to happen. Believing in His Word and hearing His voice is what will bring you into an intimate, close-knit relationship with Abba God, our heavenly Father.

From the Scriptures we learn that if we don't keep His commandments, we are liars. Let's take a look at 1 John 2:3-6: "*And hereby we do know that we know him, if we keep his commandments. He that saith, I know him, and keepeth not his commandments, is a liar, and the truth is not in him. But whoso keepeth his word, in him verily is the love of God perfected: hereby know we that we are in him. He that saith he abideth in him ought himself also so to walk, even as he walked.*" Notice it says that we should walk as He walked. To say that you are very familiar with Jesus in this context is to say that you understand His unconditional love, grace, and promises that He has for us. We should have child-like faith in all that He is. It takes a renewed mind to achieve this, something I'll be discussing in a later chapter.

When my younger son Jacob was around three years old, I remember many different moments when he would trustingly jump into my outstretched arms as I stood in a swimming pool, waiting to catch him. Due to our relationship, he had grown to trust me and to know in his heart and mind that I would catch him. Therefore, he had no fear of the water. In this same way, we, in turn, can trust and know that when we actually walk in the things God has commanded us to, such as healing the sick, we will see a favorable outcome. This is due to the personal time we spend with Him. In the book of John, it states four times "*the apostle that Jesus loves.*" John was talking about himself. Now, some would conclude from this that John was arrogant and thought himself higher than anyone else. I, however, believe that John said this only because he knew Jesus so well and had a heart revelation of how much Jesus loved him. Knowing Jesus is to know how much He loves you. As for John, he ended up being the only disciple standing at the foot of the cross at the time of Jesus' crucifixion. He was also the only one that Jesus entrusted to take care of His mother, Mary. This was all because John knew Jesus intimately and had an unshakably close relationship with Him.

If we try to convince ourselves that we have a great relationship with Jesus, when we really don't, that makes us a liar. Keeping His commandments is difficult only when we are led by our flesh and not by our spirit. At times, you may rationalize your sinful behavior or thoughts but don't realize that by doing so, you are unintentionally disobeying Him. We have all been there to some degree. To be more proactive, not only can we try taking a better look at ourselves, but we can also ask a mature, nonjudgmental Christian friend or mentor to help us figure out where we are in our relationship with Christ. Furthermore, we can also humble ourselves by asking the Holy Spirit to remove the desire to perform while replacing it with the willingness to obey the Word of God.

Look again at 1 John 2:5. Did you catch the part that says, *"the love of God perfected"*? Wow: By merely being obedient to this beautiful and loving God of ours, we can have His incredible love being perfected in us. Please stop and meditate on that verse; you will feel the presence of the Holy Spirit working in you. When we honestly believe in our heart and mind what the Bible is saying, it is, as I like to say, hallelujah time! Due to the love that God has for us, He decided to use us for this mission of changing the world, one person at a time. When we learn how to co-labor with our Lord and Savior, Jesus Christ, we will have so much more opportunity to bring about godly change in this world. Allowing us to release His power and love to others is an immense honor and privilege that He has bestowed upon us.

When I am out in public, I usually make it a point to ask the Holy Spirit for a word of knowledge for someone who needs healing in his or her body. Most of the time, I'll hear the Holy Spirit's voice clearly. The Holy Spirit will point out an individual to me that I am supposed to minister to. This is a subtle thing where I look around the room, see someone, and feel like this is the right one to minister to. Once this takes place, I will typically ask the person whether or not he or she has any pain in a particular area of his or her body. Sometimes I just know where their pain is, while other times I can feel their pain in the same area on my own body. Seldom might I get this information wrong. In these instances, the person may look at me funny and say "no" when asked about their pain. Of course this situation would make any person feel awkward, especially when they're first starting to walk in God's commandment to heal His people. However, when you get past thinking of yourself in these situations, you can feel the love of God saying that He is proud of you for stepping out and for caring more about kingdom advancements than about yourself. I don't ever want to miss out on God telling me to go and approach someone on His behalf. Therefore, I will step out even if I'm not 100% sure. Just remember: He rewards those who are obedient to Him.

In 2 Corinthians 10:5-6, Paul teaches the carnal Corinthians how to combat spiritual warfare by "*casting down imaginations, and every high thing that exalteth itself against the knowledge of God, and bringing into captivity every thought to the obedience of Christ; And having in a readiness to revenge all disobedience, when your obedience is fulfilled.*" Satan will try to convince us of all kinds of ridiculous things. He has no power over us unless we believe his lies. Resist him, and he will flee from you. As Paul says, every thought that is in rebellion to God must be made to submit to His authority in Christ Jesus. When we learn to hear His voice more consistently, we are more likely to commune with Him throughout the day. This is an easy task when we are head over heels, madly in love, with Jesus, just as He is with us. As you might well know, the process of "falling in love" with Jesus is different from romantic love.

When we first fall in love with a person romantically, we grow infatuated and cannot stop thinking about them. But over time, as we become more accustomed to their presence in our life, our once all-consuming thoughts of them can dwindle down to a minimum. On the other hand, when a relationship with Jesus is established, in the beginning we may not spend a lot of time thinking about Him. However, over time this relationship actually becomes stronger as we grow in awe of Jesus, and then we're unable to stop thinking about Him. When you apply the things that I talk about in this book in your life, this kind of a relationship with Jesus will manifest.

To obey Him, we have to know what He is telling us to do. First of all, you need to spend a lot of time in His Word and read it slowly and meditate on it. This is to help you understand it more clearly. If there is something that you don't understand, with faith ask the Holy Spirit to explain it to you. Praying in tongues after I have read the Scriptures sometimes helps me understand them more clearly. I have read the New Testament at least 30 times and the Old Testament about 3 to 4 times. There are many commandments from Jesus in the New Testament that you can follow. When you believe that you hear from the Holy Spirit, make sure it lines up with the Word of God. Furthermore, if you have indeed surrendered to Him, know that you will feel peace about it.

Don't wait for Jesus to draw closer to you — He already is. Rather, seek Him and the relationship will blossom. Hearing from God directly will give you specific direction for your life and for your walk with Him. Stop and analyze what you think God is telling you. Then spend time to figure out whether or not what you are hearing is actually from God. A lot of times it is thoughts that you would not think of yourself. If it is, then act on it. There are a lot of teachings on how to listen for His voice. Joyce Meyer has an excellent four-part series on this topic, and Andrew Wommack covers it throughout many great lessons.

The Bible is the living Word and is exceptionally inspirational to those of us who believe. Toward the end of each gospel, when it is nearing the time for Jesus to ascend to heaven, He reveals fantastic truths to believers in clear and precise words. For example, in John 14:21, He says, "*He that hath my commandments, and keepeth them, he it is that loveth me: and he that loveth me shall be loved of my Father, and I will love him, and will manifest myself to him.*" Having His commandments means that they are part of who we are rather than something that we have memorized. Memorizing Scripture is an outstanding way of renewing our minds while helping them come into agreement with the Word of God. Keeping His commandments becomes comfortable when they are a part of us because they become our belief system. Loving and worshiping Jesus in all we do is rooted in our DNA. It is the way God designed us to be. Love is the number-one addiction that mankind has, but many have directed this love towards other people and material things. God sees your heart, so don't try to fool yourself if you don't have this kind of love for Him. Ask the Holy Spirit, in faith, to help you in this area of your life. It is a request that He is happy to fulfill in you. It is glorious when He manifests Himself to us and when we are able to walk in His love and His power. Glory to God for this!

God has a way of manifesting Himself through you, to people that you encounter. A few years back, I was at a restaurant in Pasadena and asked the Lord for a word of knowledge for anyone in the restaurant. I immediately felt a slight pain in my back. I noticed a guy sitting near me in a booth and asked the Lord if the pain was his. God didn't validate my assumption. I continued scanning the room and noticed the waitress rushing past me. With excitement I asked God if the pain I felt belonged to her. I immediately felt electricity going through my hand. This was God's way of answering my question with a resounding "yes." The waitress was busy, so I had to wait for an opportune time to approach her. Eventually it was time for me to pay my bill at the cash register. This, I decided, was the perfect timing to approach the waitress about her pain. I asked her about it while visually showing her the area that I had felt the slight pain in. Stunned, she asked me how I knew this. I told her that God had told me and that He wanted to heal her. I then went on to ask her whether or not she was open to the idea of me praying for her. She laughed and said, "No, that's OK." At that moment I perceived that the Holy Spirit had told her that it was OK. It was like the Holy Spirit connected our thoughts into one and I knew it was OK, so I commanded the pain to go away "in the name of Jesus Christ." Glory to God, she said the pain was gone. Wasting no time, she eagerly asked, "You're good. Do you do fortune telling as well?" I responded, "No, this is Jesus, and He loves you. Did you know this?" She replied saying that she knew.

About a month later, I was in the same restaurant. That same waitress came over to ask me if I could pray over her headache. I did, and it went away. I am confident that the healing experiences she had made Jesus a lot more real to her. You see, God first directed me to the person with the back pain. Then, through the Holy Spirit, God instructed me to command healing in her body. I, in turn, obeyed His instruction while trusting that He would show me the way. Lastly, what Jesus had already provided on the cross manifested in her healing. All I had to do was be obedient to Him.

Obedience to God occurs when our relationship with Him is stable. In essence, this is the life that God intended us to live. He is a good Father and wants us to have the desires of our heart. In 1 John 3:22, John states, "*And whatsoever we ask, we receive of him, because we keep his commandments, and do those things that are pleasing in his sight*." We obey out of relationship and faith; therefore we receive what we ask for.

I realize that the hardest part of obedience on a personal level may not be the fact that you don't want to obey God. Instead, the most challenging part is that you simply are not sure of what He is saying. Sometimes I just wish Jesus would show up in person and tell me in plain English what to do. In His wisdom, He knows that we learn to hear His small, soft voice by seeking His presence. This way, we become more dependent on God and learn to have constant communication with Him. Fortunately we can read His commandments in the Bible and easily practice obedience.

On September 9, 2012, I felt like God was telling me to start a healing ministry. As I was pondering this, at church that day when the ministry team was praying before service, a lady in the group announced that someone in the room needed to go ahead and do what God was telling them to do. Little did she know that this "someone" was me. About three years later I started teaching healing classes and was also part of a startup healing room in Pasadena. This desire first stirred immensely and passionately in my spirit, then manifested itself into the physical realm after a lot of studying and stepping out into the healing ministry by the laying of hands on the sick. In simple terms, God first put the desire in my heart to do this and then had the lady at church relay the confirmation to me. Sometimes it might take years or decades before a word given will actually come to pass. God will lead us step by step, and I believe it will happen as soon as we are ready to take on the task and follow His direction. Initially, I didn't fully trust that it was possible for me to walk in a healing ministry, but I did know that we were not to limit God. Keep your mind set on what He can do rather than what you are capable of doing.

7

—

DILIGENTLY SEEK HIM

You have to want relationship with Him more than anything in your life!

In my opinion, to diligently seek God means to have a burning desire for an awareness of His presence throughout every waking moment. It does not mean to seek His presence here and there throughout the day. Jesus said He would never leave us or forsake us. Therefore, we merely need to be aware of His presence. I hear people sometimes say, "Let's wait for God to show up." I can't help but feel how wrong this is. We don't need to wait because He has never left us and never will. Smith Wigglesworth, one of God's Generals, had a sensational healing ministry and documented 20 people raised from the dead. Smith knew that being aware of God's presence was something he could control by keeping worldly things out of his house. As a result, he would not even allow newspapers to come into his house. The only thing that he ever read was the Bible. Smith knew that this type of dedication to Jesus would manifest into the fruit that Christ Himself experienced in his ministry. He had a fantastic level of faith that only a few in the Body of Christ have ever experienced. I believe it's because he put supreme value on Jesus Christ — and little value on everything else in the world.

Here's an example of Smith's faith. One day in the 1800s when Smith was a passenger in another pastor's vehicle, they ran out of gas on the highway. This pastor was mortified because he was driving one of the most famous pastors in the world and had run out of gas. Smith asked him if he had any water. The pastor told him that he did. Smith then instructed him to pour the water into the vehicle's gas tank. Now, I don't pretend to know much about cars, but I'm pretty sure (as was the pastor, I bet) that water in the gas tank is not a good thing. Nevertheless, reluctantly the pastor obeyed and did as Smith instructed, and to his astonishment, Smith had turned the water into gasoline. I remember reading this and feeling so inspired that I explicitly recall my faith being increased to a whole new level. Sadly, a person can go the other way. Rather than believing it and allowing it to increase their faith, they can doubt that such a thing is humanly possible, causing their faith to remain stagnant. I choose to believe that our God is a big God and that He will reveal the truth to us as long as we are willing to believe. As Smith used to famously say, "Only believe."

As I previously mentioned, when I first became a Christian, Linda and I attended a church near Nevada City that didn't believe in God's power or that He still heals. They went as far as forbidding their congregation to speak in tongues. And it was at that time that I had received my supernatural healing in my shoulder at Bethel Church in Redding, California. I remember sharing this exciting experience with my church pastor at the time, and he responded by saying, "People don't always get healed." He was a great guy and I loved him, but he just didn't know the truth about our amazing God. Not all seminary schools teach on the fact that Jesus is the same yesterday, today, and forever. At the time, I was told on multiple occasions that I was very zealous for God. They made me think that being zealous for God was a negative and weird thing. That pastor rationalized my behavior by telling me that individuals who become Christian late in life, as I did at the age of 51, tend to be passionate and zealous with their newfound faith. What he didn't know was that the reason I was so zealous and passionate was that I was diligently seeking Him.

Watching recorded Christian shows, reading the Bible, diligently studying the Word of God, and doing studies on the Internet became a part of my life. And to add to it, through my church I also volunteered for about three years at the local county jail, ministering to inmates. Even though at the time I didn't know the Bible very well, I learned how to love the guys and gals in jail because I took Matthew 25:36 to heart. From experience I can personally tell you that when we dedicate a good portion of our time to our "Father's business," His love becomes more apparent to us, flowing through us to others. And at that time, God's love flowing through me to the inmates was exactly what they were in desperate need of, rather than a Bible scholar.

In August of 2010, the last night that I was ministering in jail in Nevada City, before moving back down to Los Angeles County, God rewarded me with a precious, great gift. After ministering to one class, I felt a prompting to go to a different area of the jail and told my friend I was going over to the "N" section. I ended up ministering to about 13 federal female prisoners. There was a young lady at the opposite end of the table from me who said that she had accepted Jesus as her Savior that morning. I told her that Jesus sent me to tell her that He was head over heels in love with her. She told me how she was a cutter (people who cut themselves with a knife or razor blade), but this moment was the first time in her life that she felt like living. All of us in the room were in tears! About 10 minutes later, another young lady asked if it was OK if she accepted Jesus, too. It couldn't get any better than this! Thank You, Jesus, for that beautiful parting gift that You gave to those ladies and me.

Later on in my Christian journey, I began to read books on the supernatural. In total I've read about 30 different books. In the beginning, it was hard to believe that I could lay hands on the sick and that they would get well. However, the more I read about it, the more I came to realize that everyone can heal the sick. *"He that believeth and is baptized shall be saved; but he that believeth not shall be damned. And these signs shall follow them that believe; In my name shall they cast out devils; they shall speak with new tongues; They shall take up serpents; and if they drink any deadly thing, it shall not hurt them; they shall lay hands on the sick, and they shall recover"* (Mark 16:17-18).

When we spend time reading about all of these miracles and how God uses His willing "vessels" to release His power into the world, this time spent brings to life what the Bible is already telling us. Our lives would be much different if from birth we weren't allowed access to worldly things such as the news, and were cut off from negative influences in school or ones that came from family and friends. And if parents not only knew the truths of the Bible but also practiced them daily while teaching and affirming them to us, these miracles that you read about in books would be effortless and frequent. You don't have to be as strict as Smith Wigglesworth, but your results will soar if you spend more time in the Word of God while believing what it says. Moreover, I suggest you study others who have walked in this level of faith while simultaneously stepping out in faith yourself. Faith without works is dead (James 2:20). However, be careful of what books you read; make sure everything you read lines up with the Word of God.

God is a rewarder of those who diligently seek Him. Hebrews 11:6 says, *"But without faith it is impossible to please him: for he that cometh to God must believe that he is, and that he is a rewarder of them that diligently seek him"*.

Yes, God has given us grace and forgiven our sins. However, He also wants us to do our part and diligently seek Him so that He can manifest His power through us.

Several years ago I attended the School of Supernatural Ministry at HRock Church. Someone asked me once, "How is it that you can walk in such an anointing?" Without thought I replied, "You have to want it more than you want anything else in your life." There were about 80 students in our class, and one evening God rewarded us all with a spectacular gift. It was the night that Brandon, a man at our church who sees angels, was teaching us. In the middle of his teaching, he saw an angel in the back of the room touching our director Pastor David Oh's chest. Then out of nowhere the scent of eucalyptus filled the room. Brandon explained that he saw three warrior angels in the back corner of the room. He said that he saw them fly across the room, and in that very moment, we all felt heat radiate from nowhere in particular, and it smelled of fire. After that, Brandon told us that three other angels had appeared in the front of the classroom, and as they flew by, we felt a cool breeze and mist that cooled the room. Then all of a sudden, gold dust started floating down out of a light fixture and fell on Kelli, the lady sitting directly in front of me.

After all this happened, as if it wasn't bewildering enough, I started to hear people whispering throughout the room. I was able to make out one of them saying that certain individuals were beginning to see and feel an oil-like substance on their hands. All of a sudden I started feeling pressure on my hands but didn't know what it was. I noticed four clear indentations on one of my hands. It was as if someone was pressing down on my hands. I went up to Brandon and asked what this was. Thinking out loud, he told me that angels only press against an individual's wrists, so, therefore, this was Jesus touching me. He said he had heard of such occurrences but had never seen it before. By now people were "slain" all over the room by the Holy Spirit. Some were lying on the floor, some sitting, some standing, but we were all basking in God's presence, and it was glorious.

After some time, I was standing with my arms stretched out before me, with my palms facing down. Then Marna, a zealous woman after God's own heart, appeared in front of me. She placed her hands under mine and said she instantly felt an electric wave zing through her spine. Amy, another God-fearing woman, standing to my right, did the same thing to me and experienced the same outcome. Others began sensing power coming out from my belly, and another lady walked up to me and said that her hands immediately filled with a thick, brown, oily substance. God's power had filled the room, heavy and thick. Sensing it in the very air we were breathing, I decided to walk around the room, imparting this to everyone. I am confident that on this day, God decided He would reward all of the students by showing them things that they have only read about but never witnessed. He is a rewarder of those who diligently seek Him. Wow, the Holy Spirit just told me while writing this book that some of you will receive this same impartation. Yay God! I want to impress on you that it is not about the gold dust or manifestations. You don't need that; you just need to want to release His power.

I understand what grace is about and that the Holy Spirit gives out spiritual gifts as He chooses. Nevertheless, I believe that the Holy Spirit gives these gifts to Christians that are on fire for God. He sees our hearts and rewards those who seek Him diligently. Why would He give spiritual gifts to individuals that are not going to step out and create kingdom advancement? Having said this, I want to reiterate that you don't need to have a gift of healing to heal people in Jesus' name. You only need to believe what the Scriptures say. You can walk in as much power that you want to, as long as you seek it with godly intentions and faith.

Let's take a look at Proverbs 25:2: "*It is the glory of God to conceal a thing: but the honour of kings is to search out a matter.*" He doesn't hide things from us but hides them for us — for our benefit. The more we obey and seek Him, the more He will reveal to us. If you look at it as a treasure hunt, you will start feeling excited when you begin to discover His truths as you go from glory to glory. Power ministry is the most exciting and fun adventure that I have ever experienced in my life.

Just yesterday, while at church I noticed a couple sitting two rows behind me. They raised their hands indicating they were new to our church and that it was their first time there. At some point, our Pastor asked those who had health problems to stand up. With this, the husband shot right out of his seat. I leaned over to him and asked him to come to the front of the church after service so that I could pray for his back. Once the service finished, I sat him down and noticed that his left leg was about half an inch shorter than the right leg. In response to this finding, in the name of Jesus Christ, I commanded his left leg to grow out even with his right leg. It grew out, and his back pain immediately went away. He and his wife were so excited about this that they asked me also to pray for her as she had some prayer requests.

You see, if I hadn't stepped out, I would have taken the glory away from God, and that is not something I ever want to do. The Bible tells us that we are all priests and kings. Respond to God's Word and take hold of the glory of kings. Search out the matter at hand. Trust me when I say that this will lead you to the most exciting times of your life.

The Scriptures tell us to ask and it will be given to us, to seek and it will be revealed to us, to knock and it will be opened for us. This has to be done in faith, but faith without works is dead. Hebrews 4:11 states, "*Let us labour therefore to enter into that rest, lest any man fall after the same example of unbelief.*" Labor is the opposite of unbelief. When we spend more time in God's Word, reading about the supernatural, learning from others that are experiencing results, and focusing on what the Bible says we can do, we enter into His rest, and it becomes easy. A life of rest is the standard Christian life where miracles become a normal part of our lives. The supernatural is part of our DNA because Jesus is in us and works through us. When we spend a lot of time studying and learning, we find our identity in Christ. Take a stand today and make the decision that you are going to enter His rest. Be more persistent, never relenting.

You might want to find an accountability partner. You and your accountability partner can help keep one another focused on the walk to "enter His rest."

8

SPIRIT, SOUL, AND BODY

You have a new, born-again Spirit!

I want to stress again that although man wrote the Bible, God inspired it. 2 Timothy 3:16 says, "*All scripture is given by inspiration of God, and is profitable for doctrine, for reproof, for correction, for instruction in righteousness.*" When I first started reading the Bible, I would skip over some verses because I didn't understand them or, for that matter, didn't believe them. It is imperative to have faith in every word that's in the Bible to reach maturity as a Christian and walk the way Jesus wants us to. The Bible states that we are made of spirit, soul, and body (1 Thessalonians 5:23). These are three separate entities that make up our complete being. Our spirit is invisible. Therefore, we can't see it or feel it. It resides inside our body. We dwell in our body, our physical structure. Our soul is our mind, emotions, and will.

I recall while reading the Bible when I first gave my heart to Jesus in 2005, a lot of the Scriptures didn't make sense to me. For example 2 Corinthians 5:17 says, "*Therefore if any man be in Christ, he is a new creature: old things are passed away; behold, all things are become new.*" Now as a newbie, immature Christian, I didn't see or feel any change in me. I still had pride, I still cussed occasionally, I didn't love everyone, and I had plenty of negative thoughts. At the time, it didn't seem like all of the "old things" had passed away as this verse states. The enemy loves to tell us lies that he knows will keep us from God's promises. Some of these lies may be statements such as "The Bible is not the complete truth," "This is not for you," "You are not worthy," and so on and so on. A question I asked myself a lot when I first received salvation was "How come we don't feel like we are a new creation at the beginning of our walk with Jesus?" I wish that someone had taken the time to explain this to me. For this reason, I've decided to do this very thing for you through the use of Scriptures.

Let's first look at our physical appearance. It does not change overnight when we first accept Jesus as our Savior. We remain the same height, weight, and even look the same as we did before our salvation. But over time, by having the Holy Spirit inside of us, some of our bad habits may start to go away, producing a healthier body, radiant skin tone, etc. Applying this same logic, our soul does not immediately change either. We learn in Romans 12:2 that we need to renew our minds. As you can imagine, renewing our minds is a process. Most new Christians might not even be familiar with this idea. Speaking from experience, this process can be a fun, exciting, rewarding, and glorious one. Let us take a closer look at how our spirit is affected by our acceptance of Jesus as our Lord.

Unlike our body, it is our spirit that becomes brand-new upon our acceptance of Christ. Ezekiel 11:19 says, "*And I will give them one heart, and I will put a new spirit within you; and I will take the stony heart out of their flesh, and will give them an heart of flesh.*" Once this change takes place, a person won't be able to feel it physically. However, at that moment we might experience peace or suddenly feel the sensation of goose bumps. Unless someone explained it to us, we would not be physically aware of this new spirit. When a change takes place in a person's physical body, we can typically feel it. The same is true for our soul because usually we are acutely aware of our minds along with the thoughts and emotions that come from our flesh. Our spirit, on the other hand, is something that we cannot feel.

When I first learned that the Almighty God had given me a custom-made spirit as He does for all of His newly saved children, I was so excited. It was not just any spirit; it was a perfect spirit made just for me. My new spirit was a pathway to save me from the sin in my life. To help you grasp this concept even more, let's take a look at Romans 6:6: "*Knowing this, that our old man is crucified with him, that the body of sin might be destroyed, that henceforth we should not serve sin.*" Our old spirit was crucified and we have a new spirit that cannot sin. Stop for a minute and ask the Holy Spirit to give you a revelation of these verses, allowing them to sink in. Open up your heart and mind to receive this life-changing truth. Take this moment to hold your hands out, palms facing upward, while allowing your carnal thoughts to come into agreement with all that you have learned thus far. Understand that you have just received an impartation — hold onto it and don't let go! Our soul can still sin, but our spirit is incapable of it. That is why we need to renew our minds, which I discuss in the next chapter.

The most crucial part of this transformation is that our new spirit is also eternal. Hebrews 10:14 says, "*For by one offering he hath perfected for ever them that are sanctified.*" The dictionary defines the word "forever" as "eternity." In other words, with salvation we are given the spirit that we'll have for eternity. Thank God that we get to keep this perfect and loving spirit for eternity! Eternity may not be a concept that our carnal minds can comprehend just yet, but with the renewing of our minds, we will one day have a better understanding of this idea. As you learn to be Spirit led, your life will change drastically. You will begin to notice kingdom advancements taking place wherever you go, and as your faith in these truths solidifies, you will experience God's glory in every situation. I like to call this next stage in our spiritual journey "hallelujah time" or "hallelujahness." (I'm pretty sure I just made up a word there!) It is most comforting to know that before starting this next stage, our spirit is considered complete, remaining the same now and forever. We will go from glory to glory when we believe these truths.

Our new spirit is one with the Lord's. 1 Corinthians 6:17 says, "*But he that is joined unto the Lord is one spirit.*" When we first accepted Jesus as our Lord and Savior, we became one spirit with Him. However, once we go to the next level in our relationship with God by completely surrendering to Him, we can better feel and experience the divine connection described in this verse. Be aware of how much God loves you and grab hold of this revelation. It is not the conditional love that we encounter in the flesh — but rather the unconditional love that only He has for us because He is the epitome of love. Stop what you're doing and feel His Spirit interceding with yours. Do this throughout the day and you will see how things will begin to change for you. Andrew Wommack has a teaching on this topic that I highly recommend. One in particular truly changed my way of thinking, and I just know that it can do the same for you. You can find them on his webpage: www.awmi.net.

9
—
RENEW THE MIND

This is an amazing journey!

After accepting Jesus as our Savior, our soul is still capable of sinning. This sin then takes shape, becoming apparent in our actions and behaviors. When we learn how to renew our mind, our carnal thoughts come into agreement with our "new" spirit. Romans 12:2 says, *"And be not conformed to this world: but be ye transformed by the renewing of your mind, that ye may prove what is that good, and acceptable, and perfect, will of God."* **Notice** how this verse is teaching us that renewing the mind is a positive thing, a good endeavor that is acceptable to God. The most important first step to achieving this is by truly believing in the fact that every word in the Bible carries unshakable, flawless truth. By doing so, we will achieve the "perfect" will of God. Jesus taught us to pray so that His will is done on earth as it is in heaven (Matthew 6:10). A mature Christian will tell you that their life has drastically changed for the better as their relationship has grown with Christ. If you dare to believe and envision this to happen in your life, it will.

When Jesus took away my heart of stone and replaced it with a soft, flesh one, an opportunity for an intimate relationship with Him became possible. It was something I had never experienced. My new heart enables me to love and trust Him. He first starts the process of making us a new "creation" by the softening and melting of our hearts for the Lord. He then moves His way to the renewal of our minds, which is a journey in and of itself. Moreover, it helps us eventually to achieve our goal of bringing every captive thought into obedience to Jesus Christ. The key is to know that this is possible. Therefore, I strongly suggest that you desire and pursue it with fervor. Ask the Holy Spirit to help you with this process, and listen to what He says.

Throughout the years, in my pursuit of maintaining a relationship with God, the one-on-one time spent with Him has genuinely benefited me in many ways. It can and will do the same for you, too. There are different moments throughout your day that you can devote to God. I prefer to do this when there is nobody around, in complete silence, with my eyes closed shut. Sometimes I ask Him what it is that He wants to tell me for that day. Other times I'll ask God how I can better serve Him. Once in a while He might reveal answers to some of my pressing questions by giving me physical signs. These are things you can do as well. Our Lord speaks to us in different ways. While some might experience God's presence emotionally, others, like me, may have a physical experience. For example, I feel an increase of pressure in the palm of my hands or a sensation of electricity surging through my hands. As far as God's communication with me goes, I firmly believe that the physical signs He gives me are His way of nudging me towards the direction He wants me to take. I pray that this same thing will happen to you as well.

There are moments when God's thoughts bubble up from our belly, where the Holy Spirit resides. Proverbs 20:27 says, "The spirit of man is the candle of the LORD, searching all the inward parts of the belly." God's Spirit bears witness with ours and lives within every one of us (Romans 8:16). Therefore, we need to be still and hear His voice from inside of ourselves. I believe that when we ask in faith and pursue Him wholeheartedly, anything is possible. I also highly recommend that you try keeping a journal of all the things you hear God speaking to your heart. It just may come in handy one day. Here are some ways that journaling can benefit you: It may assist you in accomplishing something as big as writing your very own book. You will also have an opportunity to re-read your words, allowing you to refresh your memory. Furthermore, keeping a journal can help you continue the growth of your mind and thoughts. It can help you go back to different moments of writing to see how you have progressed and how you can help encourage yourself in your present life.

Once we learn to hear God's voice and are confident in this ability, God can easily renew our mind. The apostle Paul spent three years alone with God. It is where he first learned to hear God's voice. As seen in Galatians 1:16-18, where Paul says, "*To reveal his Son in me, that I might preach him among the heathen; immediately I conferred not with flesh and blood: Neither went I up to Jerusalem to them which were apostles before me; but I went into Arabia, and returned again unto Damascus. Then after three years I went up to Jerusalem to see Peter, and abode with him fifteen days.*" Because I know that sometimes it can become frustrating trying to hear God's gentle voice, I will guide you through this process throughout the next chapter.

As I have already stated, there have been many times when I hoped that God would show up in person and just tell me in plain English what He wanted me to do. I think that one of the reasons God doesn't speak to us in an audible voice is that He does not want puppets. Our heavenly Father wants us to love and obey Him on our own free will. If we completely surrender ourselves to God, we will gain the ability to transform our thoughts every time He speaks directly to our spirit. Pursue this alteration of your mind fervently, as it will help you develop a better relationship with Him. In turn, your confidence to hear Him will continue to grow. Keep in mind, as with all good things, it will take time, effort, patience, and faith. But above all, do not give up — for the results will be well worth it.

We can learn so much from Apostle Paul's writings in the New Testament. One of my favorite Scriptures is 1 Corinthians 2:2: "*For I determined not to know any thing among you, save Jesus Christ, and him crucified.*" In his day, Paul's focus on Jesus allowed him to be such a great apostle to so many. This focus enabled him to endure through the toughest tribulations that he experienced during his time in prison as well as others. It is still the case today. God's Word is sharper than a two-edged sword. Every time I read this Scripture, it cuts me to the core, and I love it. Read the Bible with an open heart, and you, too, will experience a fantastic transformation and renewal of your soul.

A long while ago, for a couple of years, I prayed almost every day asking the Holy Spirit to make my mind submissive to His will. I also prayed for an increase of wisdom in my life. When I asked God how I could renew my mind, He reminded me of when Mary and Joseph lost track of Jesus for a couple of days and how it upset them. Once they found Him, the two together asked Jesus why He would do such a thing, knowing how upset it would make them. He replied, "*How is it that ye sought me? wist ye not that I must be about my Father's business?*" (Luke 2:49). What this meant to me is that as we go about our daily lives, we need to keep our focus on Him and always be about our Father's business. Pray and seek these things wholeheartedly; He will answer you.

In trying to keep God as my primary focus, I strive to do His will in all the things I do throughout my day. For example, on my way to church yesterday, I stopped by the pet store to pick up some treats for our dog, Pico. I showed the employee a picture of the treat my wife had sent to my phone. The employee helped me find the treat, and we began walking towards the counter together. I could sense Jesus in her, so I told her that. In response to this, she explained that she had been a Christian her whole life. To further do what God has called us to, I asked her if she needed healing in her body. She said she didn't. Afterward, I hugged her and expressed godly love for her. She replied that she loved me, too. You see, God has called us to love one another as He has loved us (John 13:34). Although you may have thought there was going to be a healing, God gave this lady a different type of gift that day. He gave her an impartation of His love through me as I was going about my Father's business. When we are faithful in the smaller things, God will start to trust us with the bigger ones.

The following Sunday, when I got to church, the first thing I did was to save a couple of seats for my wife as I usually do. I then walked out into the lobby to look for people I felt might need prayer. An elderly lady about 90 years of age was having a hard time walking up the three steps into the sanctuary. I offered her my arm as she walked up the steps. Following my hunch, I asked her whether or not she felt any pain. She said that she mostly felt pain in her right leg. I then proceeded to ask her if I could pray for it. With a positive response, I commanded the pain to leave in the name of Jesus Christ. Praise God, she reported her pain went away! She excitedly hugged me and walked over to her seat. I later found out she was our friend's mother.

After the service, I took my place on the ministry team up front as usual. One of the individuals I ministered to had some emotional problems and asked me for prayer. She was hoping to receive a word of knowledge to help give her closure on whatever emotions she was experiencing. As I began to pray for this woman, God gave me a word that He wanted me to share with her. With this, I went on to explain to her that when she was four or five years old, something had happened to her that changed her life. Thinking back, she expressed to me that when she was four, her mother had been diagnosed with cancer. Due to her mother's condition, she was whisked away from her mom and placed in the care of others. At that moment, the Holy Spirit informed me that she carried resentment for her mother because she felt abandoned by her, and if she would just forgive her mom, all of her emotional pain would leave her. After sharing this information with her, followed by prayer, we hugged and she was able to walk away content, happy, and — most important of all — at peace.

The next lady I prayed for had back and shoulder problems. I sat her down to measure her legs. I first prayed for the left leg to grow out equal in length to the right leg, all in the name of Jesus. Afterward, she expressed that she had pain in her shoulder and upper back, so I prayed over it, too. Glory to God, all of her pain went away. Soon after, another lady walked up to me, explaining that she had pain in her left knee. With this, I sat her down and measured her legs to find out which one was shorter in length than the other. As usual practice, I prayed for her left leg to grow and to become equal in length to the right leg. She reported that she could feel her hip shift. At that moment, God had adjusted whatever needed adjusting in her body to ultimately help relieve her of the pain she had initially felt in her knee. Up until now, I have personally seen so many individuals healed of their aches, pains, and diseases that I honestly can't remember them all. I pray that you, too, will get to that point. All it takes is to make God the center of everything you do and to put yourself out there.

Romans 10:17 says, "*So then faith cometh by hearing, and hearing by the word of God.*" I have read the New Testament about 30 times, reading it slower each time to fully ingest and digest every kernel and nugget of truth — because each time around there is undoubtedly something I overlooked the previous time. I guess that's why it's called the Living Word of God. It truly is alive. Other than reading the Bible, I also try learning from others who live impactful lives with Jesus. If you have DVR, you may want to start recording the program "Praise The Lord" on TBN. It's my favorite program to record and watch. Or just try recording any pastor on Christian television that you learn from and enjoy. My all-time favorite is Andrew Wommack. You can buy his teachings and also download some of them for free on his website. Todd White's videos, also found online, are very inspirational to watch. Overall, just remember that it's entirely acceptable to honor certain people, but don't ever idolize them. The Father, Son, and Holy Spirit are the only ones you may go beyond honoring, to exalt and worship.

If ISIS or some other radical hate group raised us, we would develop those same hateful attitudes ourselves. When in school, we (hopefully) learned to keep ourselves away from bad influences as well as the wrong crowds. As adults, we need to continue guarding our hearts in this same manner. The kind of shows we watch, the things we read, and the friends we choose to surround ourselves with can influence us either positively or negatively. That's why spending a good amount of time in the Word daily — whether by reading it or listening to it — is so important. Doing this creates a perfect environment for the positive renewing of our mind. Try living out these new habits for a couple of weeks, and the things that you gave up will become less important to you. You will begin to desire more of God's

Word and, in turn, will partake in more godly activities. Jesus wasn't kidding when He said, "*When you give up your life, you will gain it.*"

When we delve deeper into the Bible, we start to see who we are. The living Word transforms our minds into becoming the good, acceptable, and perfect will of God. A mind not renewed is set on the flesh and is at war with God, but a renewed mind demonstrates the will of God. Romans 8:7-8 says, "*Because the carnal mind is enmity against God: for it is not subject to the law of God, neither indeed can be. So then they that are in the flesh cannot please God.*" Renewing our minds means that we must be aware of our thoughts at all times. We have a conscious and unconscious part of our mind. The unconscious part of our mind works much faster and takes in much more information than the conscious part. It is for this very reason that advertising works so well. Advertisements transmit information to the unconscious part of our mind. The more we see these ads, the more our brain believes them to be true. Thoughts that come into our mind need to be processed and either accepted or rejected. Anytime you have an ungodly thought, start the process to reject it. Be aware of your thoughts and change them before they manifest into sin. Once you have come to a point where you are completely aware of your thoughts, you will be able to bring them into obedience to Jesus Christ. As Proverbs 23:7 says, "*For as he thinketh in his heart, so is he.*"

Meditating on His Word is a great way not only to renew the mind but also to create revelation in your heart of who you are in Christ. I read somewhere that about 80% of the thoughts that go through our minds are negative. Meditating is simply thinking, which all of us do all day long. Meditate on John 14:12 like this (I will use myself in this example): Jesus said, "Darrell, you believe in me"; let this roll over in your mind several times for as long as you can. "The works that I do, Darrell, you will do also and greater works." Wow, Jesus told me personally that I will do the same works as Him and greater! If you do this enough, you will have a heart and mind revelation of all the healings that Jesus will use you for.

Recently I started meditating on Ephesians 3:19: "*And to know the love of Christ, which passeth knowledge, that ye might be filled with all the fulness of God.*" This is an amazing Scripture that will transform your life. When you meditate on it, allow your mind to be open and His other truths will come to mind. Some of the Scriptural truths that come to mind are "I can do all things through Christ who strengthens me," "He no longer sees my sins," "I am made righteous through Jesus Christ," "He will never leave me or forsake me." Memorize this Scripture and meditate on it every day for months. When you receive the revelation of how much He loves you, you will be filled with all the fullness of God.

10
—
WALK BY THE SPIRIT

This is how God intended for us to walk!

Let's explore why we should walk by the Spirit. The obvious reasons are that God created the universe and all of us in it, and He knows all things. When I used to volunteer in a jail ministry, I would start my sessions by asking the guys a fundamental question: "Should we trust in our understanding, or trust in a God who created all things and can hold the universe in the palm of His hand?"

To explain further, when a person thinks they should trust in their own understanding, they are indirectly choosing not to follow God's lead. Therefore, this person is less likely to believe in the fact that God is who our Bible says He is. Take the time and ask yourself if you really trust in the Lord. Find out where your heart lies. Depending on your answer, you may want to ask the Holy Spirit to reveal God's identity to you. Thankfully, we can always rely on the Holy Spirit to share truths with us anytime we ask Him to. In such instances, admit that the flesh is weak, and ask God for help in walking by the new spirit, trusting that it is of God and that He will lead us to believe in our hearts. Proverbs 3:5 says, "*Trust in the LORD with all thine heart; and lean not unto thine own understanding.*" Without this revelation, it can be difficult to walk by the Spirit. However, be encouraged that you can do this because all things are possible with God!

Walking by the Spirit requires focused effort. We need to take control of our thoughts and analyze what we are thinking. Ask the Holy Spirit what to do regarding all of the critical things that are going on in your life. Make a list of them and go to God for any answers you may need. Practice this on a daily basis, and you will continue to get better at it. Journal what He is telling you so you can go back and examine your progress in hearing His voice. If you believe that you can do this, doing it will actually become much easier.

Last weekend, I volunteered for the ministry team at an Andrew Wommack conference. The way in which I was able to join this team was by being a partner of his ministry and taking a required test to make sure that I was qualified. On the last night of the conference, Andrew called out some words of knowledge that he received for certain individuals attending that night. One of the words of knowledge was for people with back problems. In response a lady came up to me, as she was one of the people whom he had called out. She was an older woman in her mid-70s who was being a little stubborn about how I should pray for her. I got a word of knowledge that her left leg was shorter than her right and that if I sat her down to grow it out, her pain would go away. The woman was with her daughter and granddaughter, and considering her age and stubborn attitude, I looked to them with pleading eyes, hoping they would help me convince her to listen to me. Amused at the situation, the two ladies seemed to be smirking while shaking their heads. Seeking the Holy Spirit for guidance, I felt a nudge in my heart to approach the matter a bit differently. I started by telling her that I loved her and asked her if she felt the same about me. She didn't answer, so I decided to take the next step by sitting her down as I had first asked her to do. I then gently asked her to please sit square against the back of the chair as I lifted her legs up by her feet.

You see, to conduct this sort of healing on an individual, you always want to look at the heels to find out which leg is shorter than the other. I then proceeded to command the left leg to grow out even with the right leg, and it did. I then asked her to please get up and walk around. In doing so, I knew that her back pain would go away. She did as I asked and, to my surprise, what was once a frown turned into a huge smile because her pain was gone. She finally answered me back with an "I love you, too." It goes without saying that if I hadn't listened to the Spirit and was more concerned with her judgment of me, none of this would have happened.

Romans 8:5 says, "*For they that are after the flesh do mind the things of the flesh; but they that are after the Spirit the things of the Spirit.*" We will have a clear picture of what real Christian life looks like once we lose the fear of man and step out to follow the Holy Spirit. Take a hard look at how you go about your daily life. Be honest and ask yourself if you are being led by the Spirit or by the flesh. Read Romans 7 and 8, and make it a point to live a life representative of Romans 8. Surrender to the Word of God and allow it to enter your heart, becoming one with you. Remember: It is the living Word and it is sharper than a two-edged sword. It is your identity — embrace it.

The Holy Spirit's voice is a lot more authoritative than our own. His voice isn't an audible one but rather one that can be heard in our thoughts. It feels as though He is prodding our thoughts ultimately to nudge us in the direction that He wants us to take. These are not carnal thoughts but rather His thoughts. The Holy Spirit speaks to all of us. All we have to do is spend one-on-one time with Him, expecting something great to come out of it and believing that He'll speak to us. Many are looking for the spectacular and miss out on the supernatural. I love my time alone with the Holy Spirit. I always walk away with overflowing peace and confidence, knowing He is with me. Paul spent three years of one-on-one time with the Holy Spirit before attempting his ministry, as can be seen in Galatians 1:16-18. That's how important this concept of spending time alone with God is. You probably don't have the luxury of dropping everything for three years for one-on-one time, but try to spend as much time alone with Him as possible. The fullness of Christ flows through you once you can hear His voice. Renew the mind by receiving His thoughts, and before you know it, you will have adopted them, making them your own. Look at Peter's words in 2 Peter 3:16-17: "*As also in all his epistles, speaking in them of these things; in which are some things hard to be understood, which they that are unlearned and unstable wrest, as they do also the other scriptures, unto their own destruction. Ye therefore, beloved, seeing ye know these things before, beware lest ye also, being led away with the error of the wicked, fall from your own stedfastness.*" Did you get that? Peter said the things that Paul said are hard to understand. Paul never saw Jesus in the flesh but received a greater revelation in the Spirit than even the ones who physically walked with Jesus for over three years. You have the same Spirit and can receive amazing revelation in your alone time with God!

To be Spirit led means that your spirit is dominant over your carnal mind. It will take time and effort to achieve this lifestyle. In the beginning, God gave dominion to Adam and Eve. Genesis 1:28 says, "*And God blessed them, and God said unto them, Be fruitful, and multiply, and replenish the earth, and subdue it: and have dominion over the fish of the sea, and over the fowl of the air, and over every living thing that moveth upon the earth."* **God created humans to be dominant over every living thing on earth. Sadly, we lost that dominance when Adam and Eve ate the fruit from the tree of the knowledge of good and evil. Satan craftily deceived them so that they would lose their dominance, and he, in turn, could gain it. When Jesus died on the cross, He gave us the right to take that dominance back — but only if we come to the revelation of who we are in Christ. 1 John 4:4 says,** *"Ye are of God, little children, and have overcome them: because greater is he that is in you, than he that is in the world."* **Meditate on this verse and ask the Holy Spirit to bring this revelation into your heart.**

Satan has no power over us unless we believe his lies. It is easy to cast out demons because I understand the fact that "He who is in me is greater than he who is in the world." When you come to this revelation, walking in the supernatural becomes effortless. Focus on the Word of God and who it says you are. Let the Word illuminate and dominate your thoughts rather than your feelings. Our feelings deceive us, while the Word, the truth, sets us free from ourselves. Some of the misconceived notions that churches tend to believe in will be exposed by the Spirit of God. An example of this is an incorrect belief that all signs and wonders stopped after Jesus' apostles passed away. If this were true, then I must be hallucinating all of these hundreds of healing miracles that are a part of my everyday life. As I write this chapter today (February 14, 2018), I have already seen about 50 to 60 healing miracles just in the first month and a half of the year so far. No, I am not fantasizing their occurrence. And no, I am not a religious fanatic by any means. But what I am is simply a follower of Jesus Christ.

Walking by the Spirit requires constant denial of human

thoughts, such as being offended by others. People don't usually mean to hurt you. They are just doing what they think is right.
Some people honestly do not understand what it means to walk
as Jesus walked. Being offended by others is a choice, and we
should choose not to be offended, but rather to see if we can
help them in their walk with Christ. There are many advantages
of walking by the Spirit, such as genuinely being able to enjoy
the fruits of the Spirit. To that point, Galatians 5:22-23 says, "*But
the fruit of the Spirit is love, joy, peace, longsuffering, gentleness,
goodness, faith, meekness, temperance: against such there is no
law.*"

Another advantage is to be able to minister to people with
the truth rather than telling them what you think they want to
hear. Our flesh is usually fearful of saying things that people
may find offensive or frown upon. We should always minister in
love as Jesus did. If you are at all familiar with the four gospels,
you at least know that to all the people Jesus ministered to,
He was loving, yet firm. As an example, let's take a look at His
response to His disciples when they weren't able to cast the demon out of a man's son in Matthew 17:17: "*Then Jesus answered
and said, O faithless and perverse generation, how long shall I be
with you? how long shall I suffer you? bring him hither to me.*"

Sometimes, after having attempted to heal an individual, the
Holy Spirit will reveal to me that their unbelief is not allowing
them to receive their healing. In these instances, I have to be
able to let them know how to work on their faith and to let them
know how to do that in a direct, yet loving manner. I usually
direct them to Romans 10:17: "*So then faith cometh by hearing,
and hearing by the word of God.*" I also point them to Jude 1:20,
which says, "*But ye, beloved, building up yourselves on your most
holy faith, praying in the Holy Ghost.*" The next verse continues
with the admonishment to "*Keep yourselves in the love of God.*"

God always loves us, but when you have the revelation of just how much He loves you, it becomes easy to receive His healing and blessings. Most people don't want to hear that they don't have enough faith. However, if they can humble themselves to this truth, they can grow in their relationship with Jesus. I sometimes also have them quote Mark 9:24: "*Lord, I believe; help thou mine unbelief.*" I quote this myself sometimes; we can all use more belief. Go ahead and say it right now in simple English: "Lord, I believe. Help me with my unbelief." You have faith, but your unbelief can sometimes counterbalance your faith.

Walking by the Spirit can be rewarding through the things that this experience reveals to us. Going through my journal, I found an entry from October 5, 2013: I was working out on my elliptical machine, worshipping God and feeling His love and presence. A vision of a goose appeared in my mind, and I asked the Holy Spirit what this was. He told me that this was a goose with golden eggs and that He was going to bless me. Then He sent me an angel of revelation and beauty to reveal the deep secrets of God. You see, God shares all kinds of secrets with us as long as we believe Him and seek Him. Daniel 2:22 says, "*He revealeth the deep and secret things: he knoweth what is in the darkness, and the light dwelleth with him.*"

This revelation was about five years ago, and I have gone through some tough times financially since then. God knew I was going to go through those tough times. He gave me this revelation so that I wouldn't lose hope, knowing that His blessings would come with my belief in this very thing. Had I fully embraced and believed this encounter, I would have gone through the tough times a lot easier, but unfortunately, that was not the case in the beginning.

When we walk in the Spirit, we walk in His perfect love rather than our own selfish love. Ephesians 5:2 says, "*And walk in love, as Christ also hath loved us, and hath given himself for us an offering and a sacrifice to God for a sweet smelling savour.*" I believe that I have given you enough reasons of why we should walk in the Spirit and the benefits of it. You now may be wondering how we can go about walking in the Spirit. First and foremost, your desire to want a relationship with the Holy Spirit — more than your desire for anything else — will lead you to victory in this area. John 15:5 says, "*I am the vine, ye are the branches: He that abideth in me, and I in him, the same bringeth forth much fruit: for without me ye can do nothing.*" From this verse, we know that we are not without Him and that He will never leave us or forsake us.

In those quiet moments that we spend with the Holy Spirit, we learn how to hear His voice. Block your carnal mind and receive His wisdom and His desire for your life. Believe what the Bible says in John 10:27: "*My sheep hear my voice, and I know them, and they follow me.*" Satan will tell you that hearing from God is only for the "super sheep." There are no super sheep. We are all made in His image and can hear from Him. He has given us a new spirit and heart. God wants you to hear from Him more than you want to. When we seek Him with all of our heart and soul, our love for Him increases, and that is what He truly wants.

As we grow in our relationship with Jesus, we learn to hear His small, quiet voice. John 16:29 says, "*His disciples said unto him, Lo, now speakest thou plainly, and speakest no proverb.*" He is speaking plainly to us now, but if I am expecting to hear a shout, a parable, or something else that's even more dramatic, I will miss out on what the Holy Spirit is telling me. Without a doubt, He wants you to hear His voice. However, we have to go about it in the right way, scripturally. God has set-up both spiritual and physical laws, and there is no way around them. Meditate on the Scriptures in this chapter and believe. When you get good at hearing from the Spirit, it changes how you minister to others.

One day, as I was serving on the ministry team at church, the Holy Spirit led me to some astounding truths. While ministering to the first gentleman who approached me, I received a revelation from the Holy Spirit that this guy had a "spirit of witchcraft" on him and that it was from New Orleans. He said that his parents were from Louisiana. With that revelation, I was able to minister to him accordingly. The second person I ministered to was a young man about 16 years of age. Based on what the Holy Spirit revealed to me, I told him that his father left him when he was four years old, and he confirmed this. I explained to him that his heavenly Father cared so much for him that He revealed this truth to me, so that I can minister to him over this area of his life. The third person I ministered to was a lady who had a spirit of Buddhism on her. She confirmed that she used to practice Buddhism and, once again, with this revelation I was able to minister to her over that area of her life. When we share these truths with others, it allows them to see that not only does God know what they have been through, but also that He cares enough to send someone to minister to them.

A hardened heart can be a hindrance in hearing from God. This kind of heart can come from sin, but it can also come from not keeping our minds focused on things of the Spirit, as it states in Romans 8:5. If I spend all my spare time watching TV shows that are not focusing on God or other things that occupy my time, I am not thinking of things of the Spirit. We need to focus on the things of God as much as possible. The more time spent in the Word, meditating on the Word, or alone time with God will result in hearing from Him and walking by the Spirit.

Set your mind on the things of the Spirit and not on the

things of the flesh. Place more value on God than any other area of your life, even family. This properly placed value will lead to being Spirit-led, and you will overcome all the roadblocks that Satan has placed in your life. When we have achieved this, all the bad things that happen in our lives will not have a negative impact on us. Then you will be able to walk as Jesus walked, as 1 John 2:6 declares, "*He that saith he abideth in him ought himself also so to walk, even as he walked.*" Every word in the Bible is absolute truth. Please keep this simple. Spend alone time with God, meditate on His Word, focus on Him, believe that you can be Spirit led, and desire it more than anything in your life.

When you learn to be Spirit led, things like this will happen to you. My wife and I were in Colorado Springs, visiting my brother Bill and his wife, Penny. We were at Seven Falls, doing what tourists do. As I was waiting in this outside area for my wife to finish eating, I asked the Lord who He wanted me to minister to. I felt like it was these two ladies about 20 feet from me. So I approached and asked the one lady if she had a problem with her neck. They looked at each other in astonishment. This is the email that she sent me later that day:

> "*I am the woman God led you to today at 7 Falls. I want to thank you for listening to God's voice and obeying His direction. Words cannot describe what a difference you allowed God to make in my health. I have been pain free all day with no muscle contraction whatsoever. It has been a long road for me since the Mac truck rear ended me in August 1999. I have spent endless days in bed, drugged to dull the pain of migraines, and many times thought it would be easier to end my life than to endure one more second of pain. Over the years I have spent thousands of dollars in search of a cure, I have asked God for healing and finally came to the conclusion, and this was my*

cross to bear. This morning when I woke with a migraine, I wondered how I would make a 9 hour trip home tomorrow. I figured it would entail more pain killers and hours of grueling pain. Thank you for opening your heart to God's leading!!

You mentioned teaching a class in February and I am very much interested. I will check out your website and look forward to hearing God's word and direction!

blessings,"

I asked her if I could use her testimony, and here is her reply:

"Absolutely you may use my testimony! And I have already shared my story with several people and given your information to a friend.

I have felt Satan's attacks 3-4 times since the Lord healed me. Pain will start to flare and all I have to do is claim the healing and it's gone. Sweet! The Lord is so incredibly good!

I have marked my calendar in Feb to start watching your website for your class. I have 2 other people wanting to take it with me so I'm very excited!

love & blessings,"

I just got off the phone with this lady, Jana, to see how she is doing three months later. She is still pain free and praising God! She said it was amazing that God had told me about her neck and that I came over to get her healed. It made her feel that God sees her on a personal level. She was excited and felt loved that God was reaching out and touching her. Of course she will be ministering God's power to others in the future.

ALL THE GLORY TO GOD!!!

11
—
KNOW WHO YOU ARE IN CHRIST

Your DNA is that of Jesus Christ!

On the morning of August 24, 2015, during my intimate time with God, the Holy Spirit showed me a vision and then helped me understand what it meant. I saw an hourglass that had just been turned upside down by someone. The sand had begun to flow downward, through its neck, and into the bottom half. This vision was a representation of what it is like to become a new Christian. To explain, I realized that the "process" of becoming a born-again Christian should start from the moment we begin renewing our minds. Like the hourglass, this process has a start and an end. However, unlike the hourglass's steady, timed 60 minutes, gaining a different perspective can be as slow or fast as you allow it to be.

Renewing one's mind occurs through the help of positive role models as well as, of course, reading the Word of God. These role models should be individuals who not only help us become mature Christians but also help us understand who we are in Christ. Most of us haven't had the privilege of having good mentors guiding us in this process. Something I would suggest for you to take part in would be a "Discipleship Program." Your church may have such a program, but if not, I would advise you to look for one elsewhere. Either way, it is imperative you find one that is led by humble individuals who believe in everything the Bible says. It will help you learn from them while giving you the opportunity to contribute to their growth as well.

Galatians 4:7 says, "*Wherefore thou art no more a servant, but a son; and if a son, then an heir of God through Christ.*" We are sons and daughters of Almighty God. Take a moment and let this verse sink into your heart and mind. Reflect on how amazing this fact is. When you grasp this idea, you will never again be the same. Jesus wasn't kidding when He said, "*When you give up your life, you gain it.*" Let this really sink in: "*an heir of God through Christ.*" A RADICAL STATEMENT! I know that my flesh is no good and I fall short of the glory of God. However, I also know that I am a new creation in Christ. 2 Corinthians 5:17 states, "*Therefore if any man be in Christ, he is a new creature: old things are passed away; behold, all things are become new.*" So, I don't concentrate on the fact that I am not worthy (through my flesh) — but instead that I am a new creation and can do all things through Christ. The enemy wants me to think that I am not worthy. But I am worthy because I am a co-labor of Jesus Christ. I am royalty. And you are, too! Embrace your new identity as a co-laborer and forget about the old you.

To help you get to where you need to be, I'm going to use the parable of the sower in Luke 8:5-8: "*A sower went out to sow his seed: and as he sowed, some fell by the way side; and it was trodden down, and the fowls of the air devoured it. And some fell upon a rock; and as soon as it was sprung up, it withered away, because it lacked moisture. And some fell among thorns; and the thorns sprang up with it, and choked it. And other fell on good ground, and sprang up, and bare fruit an hundredfold. And when he had said these things, he cried, He that hath ears to hear, let him hear."*

Later on in the chapter, in verses 11 to 15, Jesus explains how the devil comes and takes away the Word out of our hearts. He goes on to demonstrate how others believe the Word for a short while and then how they fall away from it as soon as they run into temptation. In these verses Jesus illustrates how the cares of the world and the riches and pleasures of life deceive some individuals. In turn, they bring no fruit to maturity. He ends these verses by saying, "*But that on the good ground are they, which in an honest and good heart, having heard the word, keep it, and bring forth fruit with patience."*

When Jesus shared this parable with the multitude, His specific words in verse 8 were "*He who has ears, let him hear."* Everybody has ears, but He was speaking to those who would heed His Word and walk it out accordingly. In verse 15 He refers to individuals who have a good and noble heart that is surrendered and dedicated to believing the Word of God, as the seed that fell on the right ground. This is not just for pastors, biblical scholars, or a few chosen people. God shows no partiality and will manifest Himself to anyone who will dare to believe His Word. I ask that you please meditate on this verse and see yourself as the good ground with a noble and perfect heart. You were made in His image. He just told me that He loves you very much — more than you can ever comprehend! All that you have done in the past was forgiven by God the moment you asked for His forgiveness. God has made you into a new creation in Christ Jesus, His Son. When you give up being who you were in the past, you can move forward in fulfilling God's desire for us, the desire to release the living Christ to the dying world.

Having revelation about this parable allows us to honestly

know who we are in Christ, and once that happens, the cares of this world will begin to have less and less effect on us. Our friends that are negative or not wanting to take the same path of truth will eventually play a diminished role in our lives. God will bring new people into our lives to help us with our walk. Ask Him for the wisdom to choose the right people to associate with. Seek His advice on what Bible study group or church you should be a part of. Being in a positive, godly environment will help you grasp the fact that you are "good ground" and that you have a great heart. Thus, the seed that has been sown in your good ground will begin to sprout and bloom and bear wonderful fruit.

The entire Bible points to the love and goodness of Jesus and reveals that we are no longer called servants, but friends and co-laborers of Christ Himself. The 12 named disciples from the Bible weren't the only individuals chosen by Him. He has also picked you and knows that you, too, will be one of His amazing disciples. In fact, I'm going to go as far as saying that if you would have lived 2,000 years ago, you, too, may have been in the Bible. I suggest this only because I know that God believes in you and has a great purpose for your life. Romans 12:2 explains God's perfect will for us. Allow Him to lead you step by step into this revelation with a patient and trusting heart.

In Matthew 14, the disciples tell Jesus to send the multitude away so they can go into town to buy themselves food to eat. Jesus responds, "*They need not depart; give ye them to eat*" (Matthew 14:16). The disciples become puzzled by these instructions; they wonder how they're supposed to give the multitude something to eat when all they have are five loaves of bread and two fish. The Bible says in Matthew 14:19-21, "*And he commanded the multitude to sit down on the grass, and took the five loaves, and the two fishes, and looking up to heaven, he blessed, and brake, and gave the loaves to his disciples, and the disciples to the multitude. And they did all eat, and were filled: and they took up of the fragments that remained twelve baskets full. And they that had eaten were about five thousand men, beside women and children."* Notice how it was the disciples that passed the food out to the multitude.

Later, in Matthew 16, when Jesus told His disciples to, *"Take heed and beware of the leaven of the Pharisees and of the Sadducees,"* they thought He was talking about the fact that they didn't bring any bread along for the journey. He then said, *"Do ye not yet understand, neither remember the five loaves of the five thousand, and how many baskets ye took up?"* (Matthew 16:9). You see, although Jesus' disciples were physically walking with Him, they hadn't received the revelation of who they were in Christ. Supernaturally, Jesus could have commanded bread to show up in front of each person, but He chose to use His disciples to be a part of the miracle. Today He wants you to be a part of miracles, too. Keep in mind that this all took place before Jesus died on the cross — before they officially received their power from God in Acts 2, when the Holy Spirit came upon them. You have an amazing advantage living in the time you live in now, after the cross. You are about to begin on a journey that will forever change your life and the lives around you. Your identity is in Christ!

The more we study the Word of God, the more our faith and understanding will grow. With this, we will begin to grasp the fact that the moment we received the baptism of the Holy Spirit, we were immediately given power from above to walk out God's kingdom here on earth. Understand that ultimately, God chose you and me to be a part of His miracles today.

I once prayed for a lady who had to use hearing aids to be

able to hear. I told her to take them out and informed her that she was not going to need them anymore. She took out her hearing aids, and when I asked her if she could hear me, it was clear that she couldn't because she was reading my lips. I commanded her hearing to open up in the name of Jesus. I had to do it a couple of times before it improved to the point where she was able to hear me clearly without the use of her hearing aids. Her hearing was restored! And as she went to use the restroom, her sister who was with her told me that she had some back pain. So I asked her to sit down in a chair. I noticed that her left leg was shorter than her right one, so I commanded it to grow out in the name of Jesus. It shot right out! Jolted with surprise, she jumped up and walked around as she confirmed that her back pain was gone. Right about then her sister came back from the restroom. Shaking her head and chuckling, she shared, "I don't want to sound gross, but this is the first time in my life I could actually hear toilet paper hit the water after using the toilet!" We serve a BIG GOD. It's not about us, but about making ourselves available to Him so that He can use us for kingdom advancement.

Believe in who the Bible says you are. If we believe everything that is written in the Bible, we will be able to walk in the fullness of Christ. Ephesians 1:19 says, "*And what is the exceeding greatness of his power to us-ward who believe, according to the working of his mighty power.*" Hosea 4:6 explains that His people are destroyed for lack of knowledge. You are receiving the understanding of who you are, and it is up to you to walk out this fantastic journey. He has done His part and is now waiting for you to do yours. In Galatians 2:20 we learn that in the act of accepting Jesus into our hearts, we are crucified with Christ and it is no longer we who live, but Christ who lives in us. In other words, it is not us who live in our bodies, but rather Christ who lives in us. The life that we live in the flesh, we live by faith in the Son of God, who loved us and gave Himself for us. Read these Scriptures with an open heart and let it permeate into every fiber of your being. Let the living Word transform you into His image.

In the gospel that he wrote, John refers to himself as the disciple whom Jesus loved. And he does this four different times in case we missed it the first few times. Religious people may look at him and think it was arrogant for John to say this in his own gospel. The reality is that John had a revelation of how much Jesus loved him. In the first, second, and third epistles of John, he uses the word "love" more than 25 times. Notably, the book of John is often recommended for new believers to read first because it really hones in on the love of Jesus. John was also the chosen author of the final, closing book in the Bible, the book of Revelation. All this — along with the fact that John was trusted by Jesus to care for His mother, Mary, as his own — I would say that pretty much gives him bragging rights. When we have personal knowledge of the truth such as "Jesus loves me," He will trust us with the desires that He puts into our hearts. Ask the Holy Spirit to reveal to you the width, length, depth, and height of His love for you.

Let's take a look at Ephesians 3:19: "*And to know the love of Christ, which passeth knowledge, that ye might be filled with all the fulness of God.*" Through this verse, we learn that when we know the love of Christ, we become aware of the truth that we are filled with all the fullness of God. As I stated earlier, please mediate on this verse for months to receive this revelation. Now look at Ephesians 3:20-21: "*Now unto him that is able to do exceeding abundantly above all that we ask or think, according to the power that worketh in us, Unto him be glory in the church by Christ Jesus throughout all ages, world without end. Amen.*" Let your imagination go wild and think of all the different things that we can do with the power that God has placed in us. Then recognize that God can do so much more beyond all of that. According to Romans 8:11, we have the same power in us that raised Jesus Christ from the dead. It is because of who we are in Christ that healing individuals along with walking in the supernatural becomes so easy. Understand that nothing is impossible. Demons can be readily cast out because He who is in you is greater than he who is in the world. When we know who we are in Christ, the supernatural just happens, and this is the normal Christian life. When we come to the revelation of how much God loves us, we are transformed into a powerful vessel, going about our Father's business.

2 Corinthians 10:8 says, "*For though I should boast somewhat more of our authority, which the Lord hath given us for edification, and not for your destruction, I should not be ashamed.*" He loves us so much that He allows us to minister to others with authority that He has given us, for the sole purpose of edifying them. The gospel is the good news and, although it might seem too good to be true, it is entirely and positively 100% true.

I want to take a moment to briefly touch on false humility. The "religious" Church is very much into false humility. I was in a study group one time and actually heard someone in the group make a comment along the lines of, "When I get an idea in my head about doing something big, I know that the idea must be from me and not God." I verbalized to this person how I disagreed with this thought. I explained that God wants us to do big things to help edify others as we do His works. Place your value on the truth, that you are a son or daughter of Jesus Christ.

Insecure people think that confidence is actually arrogance.

This is wrong thinking. We need to teach the timid to become confident. As long as you are making God your only resource and are giving Him all of the glory, you are humble and not arrogant. Therefore, you will be able to do all things through Christ. Humility is merely the act of being dependent on God and not yourself.

12

—

FAITH

Faith is a God-given gift!

God created us and has revealed Himself to mankind and gave us the free will to either believe or not believe the words written in the Bible. As we know, this decision has both eternal and present-day consequences. Since you are reading this book, I will assume that you have already accepted Jesus Christ as your Lord and Savior. Faith is vital in all areas of our lives. As I have discussed and shown Scriptures to back it up, faith is needed to receive many of God's blessings. God made spiritual and physical laws. He created gravity so we won't fall off the planet. This is a law that cannot be overridden without a miracle. We must abide by it, and in the same manner we comply with all other physical laws. He also made spiritual laws, and when we abide in these laws of faith, we can do the greater works that He told us we would do (see John 14:12).

An example of a spiritual law can be found in Mark 11:22-24: "*And Jesus answering saith unto them, Have faith in God. For verily I say unto you, That whosoever shall say unto this mountain, Be thou removed, and be thou cast into the sea; and shall not doubt in his heart, but shall believe that those things which he saith shall come to pass; he shall have whatsoever he saith. Therefore I say unto you, What things soever ye desire, when ye pray, believe that ye receive them, and ye shall have them."* With this knowledge, whatever we ask for in faith or command in Jesus' name will come to pass as long as it is in line with the will of God. Healing is definitely the will of God since 1 Peter 2:24 tells us that we were healed by His stripes. Also in Matthew 8:17 He states that He Himself took our infirmities and bore our sicknesses. You will come to know His will the more you study the Bible and spend time alone with Him. If you can keep it simple and believe in your heart, you will soon come to find out that the supernatural happens effortlessly. This is a spiritual law that God has put into play, and when you receive this revelation, your life will be changed forever. Living in victory is available to all of us. The most important thing we are called to do is to believe in this simple truth.

Another great example of the spiritual law of faith that God provided for us is in Matthew 9:21-22. The lady with the issue of blood for 12 years knew that if she could only touch the hem of Jesus' garment, she would be made whole. This lady risked being stoned to death by being in public in her unclean state. But her faith was so strong that she knew she would be healed. Jesus told her, *"Daughter, be of good comfort; thy faith hath made thee whole."*

A couple of weeks ago, while talking to a greeter at church named Tracy, I shared my experience of seeing three deaf ears open up at a conference I had volunteered at. In response Tracy told me that she had a friend with a deaf ear who coincidentally came to church with her that day. As the first service finished and people began to walk out, Tracy and I waited for her friend.

As her friend walked out of the service, Tracy took the initiative to formally introduce us. To provide them with some privacy, I invited the ladies to step outside with me. Excited, Tracy asked me whether or not there was anything other than praying I wanted her to do. I told her that it would be wonderful if she could agree with us in prayer. I found out that Tracy's friend had only been a Christian for two weeks and couldn't hear out of her left ear. I started out by telling her, "This is easy for God. He is going to open your ear up now." After I commanded it to be opened in the name of Jesus — glory to God — she could suddenly hear out of that ear! If I had doubted, I would have broken the spiritual law, and therefore, she would have still been deaf in that ear.

Considering she had just become a Christian merely two weeks prior, I could only imagine the kind of thoughts that might have run through her mind after having received such an amazing, miraculous healing. You might wonder how I was able to do this. Well, not only do I believe that such healing miracles are possible, but I have also come into agreement with the spiritual laws that God has placed into motion. They have become heart and mind revelations to me and are part of my thoughts and speech. When you grab hold of this revelation, the manifestations of His power will be demonstrated and released through you.

Jesus died on the cross about 2,000 years ago. He has provided salvation for those who not only believe in Him but also have faith that He is their Lord and Savior. Romans 10:9 says, *"That if thou shalt confess with thy mouth the Lord Jesus, and shalt believe in thine heart that God hath raised him from the dead, thou shalt be saved."* This is a fairly easy verse to trust in for new believers. However, it is much more difficult for them to have faith in the fact that God also provided for healing in our bodies.

Getting rid of our sicknesses and infirmities seems less spectacular than having eternal life because everlasting life promises no more suffering or tears. Although our carnal minds can't even fathom what eternity is, receiving a healing miracle can seem too good to be true. Deaf ears, blind eyes, cancer, and all other illnesses or diseases are just as manageable for God to heal, as is a simple headache. Remember: This is the same God who spoke the universe into existence. We don't need to know how He does it — just that He does! It is by His grace that healing has already been given to us. His role is grace, while our role is faith. He has already done His part, and now it is our time to do our part. Don't have faith in your goodness, but instead have faith in His unmerited favor — only then will you prosper.

When we come into agreement with spiritual laws, abundance becomes a reality in our lives. He has put all of these truths in the Bible so that we may have knowledge of them as well as gain some benefits from them. You truly get to know Him by studying His Word, believing what it says, and acting on it. Take a look at 2 Peter 1:1-3: "*Simon Peter, a servant and an apostle of Jesus Christ, to them that have obtained like precious faith with us through the righteousness of God and our Saviour Jesus Christ: Grace and peace be multiplied unto you through the knowledge of God, and of Jesus our Lord, According as his divine power hath given unto us all things that pertain unto life and godliness, through the knowledge of him that hath called us to glory and virtue.*" The knowledge given to us in the Bible can provide us with the steps needed to walk into the supernatural.

Jesus explains to us in the parable found in Matthew 25:14-30 just how the kingdom of heaven operates. In this parable, there was a man who handed his possessions to his servants before his travels. This man is a direct comparison to how God placed us on this earth and handed His "possessions" to us, i.e., spiritual gifts. In the parable, the man gave one of his servants five talents (a unit of money), to another he handed a total of two talents, and to the last one, one talent. The servant who received the five talents decided to trade them, doubling his talents. The servant who received two talents chose to follow suit, doubling his talents as well. However, the servant who received one talent decided to keep it in a safe place by burying it. When the man returned from his travels, he told the two who had doubled their possessions, "*Well done, thou good and faithful servant: thou hast been faithful over a few things, I will make thee ruler over many things.*" However, to the servant who had received one talent and had chosen to bury it, he said, "*Thou wicked and slothful servant.*" He then took the talent from him and gave it to the one who now had 10.

Matthew 25:29 says, "*For unto every one that hath shall be given, and he shall have abundance: but from him that hath not shall be taken away even that which he hath.*" All good things in life come from God and are obtained by grace through our faith and works. Our works grant us the ability to cause these spiritual laws to manifest. The more you step out and do what He commanded you to do, the more you will receive. This is just how the kingdom of God works.

What happens when we don't have faith? In James 1:6-8, we learn that he who doubts is like a wave of the sea, driven and tossed by the wind, and he who is double-minded can't expect to receive anything from the Lord. We can see an example of this portrayed in Matthew 17:19-21. Here the disciples weren't able to cure a man's son who was epileptic. Therefore, Jesus cast the demon out of him, and he was immediately healed. His disciples proceeded to ask Him why they weren't able to heal him. In response Jesus told them that it was because of their unbelief. He then explained to them that if they had faith the size of a mustard seed, they would be able to directly say to a mountain to move, and it would move. He said to them that if they had even the smallest of faith, nothing would be impossible for them. In other Scriptures, Jesus goes on to say, "*Believe in your hearts without doubting, and you will receive.*"

In Mark 9, an account of the same story, we learn that we can have belief and unbelief. We have all been given a measure of faith, but we can have unbelief creep into our thoughts. Jesus' disciples could not cast the demon out of the man's son because of unbelief. When the man came to Jesus and asked Him if he could do anything for his son, Jesus replied, "*If you can believe, all things are possible.*" The man then says, "*Lord, I believe; help me with my unbelief.*" At that moment, Jesus cast the demon out of the man's son, and he became whole.

Our unbelief can cancel out our belief. Jesus' disciples had cast out demons in the past and wanted to know why it didn't work this time. Perhaps it was because when they saw the boy fall onto the ground, convulsing and foaming at the mouth, it caused unbelief that overcame their belief. I remember one time when someone brought a lady to me with her arm all twisted up, and I prayed over it and nothing happened. I believe that the shock of seeing her arm had caused unbelief in me. In the story in Matthew 17, when the disciples asked Jesus why they could not cast the demon out, Jesus said it was because of their unbelief, but He went on to say that this kind only comes out by fasting and praying. I believe that what He was referring to was that this kind of unbelief only comes out by a lifestyle of fasting and praying.

All Christians have received a measure of faith, according to Romans 12:3. God didn't leave anyone out. He loves us all the same. The ones walking in the supernatural haven't received any more faith than you have; they only believe what the Word of God says and step out in faith to act on it. It's not faith that we lack; it's boldness. As we step out to pray for the sick and begin to see results, our faith will increase as well as our boldness. The first time I prayed for a leg to grow out, I was shocked and surprised when it did. Back then I had faith the size of a mustard seed and just a tiny bit of belief to go with it. Now every time someone complains of back pain, I immediately check the length of their legs (usually the source of back pain) and command the shorter leg to grow out in Jesus' name — and it always does! I have arrived at a place where I don't even have to command a leg to grow out; I just think about it and it grows out.

Last week I went to a hospital to pray for someone. On the way up to the room, I counted a total of six people in the elevator with me. They were a mixed group of nurses, visitors, and a doctor. Joking around with one of the nurses, I asked if I could help her make her rounds. At that moment, I suddenly got a word of knowledge about her knee. She said that she was not in pain right now, but she had problems with it. I got another word that she needed to have her leg grown out. I explained this to her and told her that if she was open to it, I could grow it out for her. During this exchange of conversation, the doctor standing in the elevator looked at me and smiled with unbelief. I smiled back enthusiastically with belief! Unfortunately, the nurse turned down my offer, but the main point I'm trying to make is the importance of being bold as I was in that elevator. I didn't care that I was in a hospital that's predominantly backed by science, or that there was a doctor in the elevator smirking. God gave me a word of knowledge as a trusted servant, so I had to obey and give it to the nurse.

I have come to a place in my walk with the Lord where I am

willing to step out of my comfort zone with boldness, even in places where people don't usually make conversation with one another. I care more about kingdom advancement than what someone will think of me, and I am honestly hoping you, too, will be encouraged to do the same. Ask yourself if you put more value on God or what other people think of you. In the kingdom of God, when we exercise our faith, we are given more. Considering this, be assured that an increase of God's blessings will come to all who step out in boldness and do what God has called them to do. Let's not bury our talents as the foolish servant did in the parable in Matthew. Instead let's step out to double them, as did the other two good and faithful servants.

Faith comes from God. It is a gift that is imparted to us by God. All you have to do is ask and believe that it's yours (Ephesians 2:8). We need to renew our minds to believe in the existence of faith, and only then will we be able to release God's power onto this earth. Satan will try to deceive us by telling us we don't have enough faith. Satan used to say to me that all those individuals I prayed for weren't really healed. In the beginning I would sometimes believe his lies. But all the testimonial emails and calls and texts I get from people telling me their pain never came back tells me otherwise. Now that I resist the devil, he doesn't even try to tell me that lie anymore. Resist the devil, and he will flee (James 4:7).

I believe that we all start out with some faith, but over time we want our faith to increase and want our belief in that faith to grow. I was teaching a class at the HRock School of Supernatural Ministry to the middle school age group a few weeks back. One of the students asked me how much faith I had in the beginning. I told her that when I was first saved, my faith wasn't steadfast. Almost immediately after, another student asked me how a person could work on increasing his or her faith. My response was Romans 10:17: *"So then faith cometh by hearing, and hearing by the word of God."* When we spend time in the Word and listen to studies about the supernatural, our faith increases. These things can help us truly grasp the idea that God is who He says He is and does what He says He can do. Over time this will help our faith increase substantially.

Depending on our upbringing, some of us have been raised to have a substantial level of faith and belief. For these individuals in particular, the supernatural will come naturally and easily because they won't even question it. We can't change the way we were raised, but we can change the influences that are in our life right now. At the end of the day, it is all dependent on how much we want to please God.

Losing the fear of man is essential to growing one's faith. Once this happens, we can start to believe in the power that God has given us. The more we step out of our comfort zone to do the things that God wants us to do, the easier it gets and the less we'll be concerned with how others view us.

A few days ago, I was at the Ontario airport. I asked the Lord for a word of knowledge for anybody of His choosing. He told me that the gentleman at a table next to me had lower back pain. So I approached him and let him know that I sensed he had lower back pain. I went on to explain that it could be because he had one leg shorter than the other. He replied that he for sure did have a shorter leg and was confident that was the cause of his back pain. As usual, I had him sit back in his chair and in Jesus' name I grew the short leg out. He got up and walked around confirming that all of his pain was gone! Again, if the fear of man had taken over me at that moment, God would not have received the glory, this man would still be in pain, and no miracle would have taken place that day.

Praying in the Spirit can also help increase our faith. Jude 1:20 says, "*But ye, beloved, building up yourselves on your most holy faith, praying in the Holy Ghost.*" Sometimes, right before church I would spend as much as two hours praying in tongues. I believe that praying in tongues helps us to be more in tune with the Holy Spirit.

James 2:20-22 says, "*But wilt thou know, O vain man, that faith without works is dead? Was not Abraham our father justified by works, when he had offered Isaac his son upon the altar? Seest thou how faith wrought with his works, and by works was faith made perfect?*" Wow, faith was made perfect by works. When we step out and heal the sick, we are perfecting our faith. With practice, healing turns into an easy task. It becomes second nature like breathing. Without putting any thought into it, healing miracles will begin to happen. All you have to do is put yourself out there. We need to get over ourselves and step out. Only then will we live and experience the normal Christian life of releasing His power and extravagant love to the world.

My job requires me to drive about two to three hours a day in grueling Los Angeles traffic. During this past month, while driving my time has been split between either listening to teachings by Andrew Wommack or praying in tongues. Since faith comes by hearing the Word of God and is increased through the act of praying in tongues, I decided to spend my time in traffic renewing my mind and growing my faith. By doing this, I have noticed an increased amount of impartation in the different spiritual gifts that I have, i.e., words of knowledge and seeing creative miracles. Not to mention a dramatic decrease in the level of stress of driving in L.A. traffic. Definitely a win-win situation!

Recently I was at a lady's house for my work and found out that she had severe back pain. I commanded her vertebrae to grow. She was shocked as she said she first felt some heat on her back and then was able actually to sense her vertebrae growing. Praise God, her pain went away! Then her 14-year-old daughter said she had a problem with her nose and went on to explain how she had a blocked passageway and needed surgery. As I commanded it to open up, she confirmed that she immediately felt air gushing through her nose. I then touched a spot on her back as I told her that I sensed she had back pain in that area. She verified that she did, so I sat her down and grew her leg out, and her pain went away. Then she shared with me that even though she studied as hard as she could, she still flunked her school exams due to poor memory retention issues. I commanded her brain to be restored, and she felt tingling going through her head. To top it off, I was able to lead her to Christ after that. What started off as another routine appointment given to me by my employer ended up being a divine appointment given to me by my God.

A few weeks ago I was at a fast food restaurant. Before I left, I asked the Holy Spirit for a word of knowledge, so He highlighted a lady in a booth near me. I went up to her and asked if she a problem with her neck. She replied that she had been in an accident and had pain in her neck. When I commanded it to leave in Jesus' name, she had a big smile on her face and confirmed that it went away. In another booth nearby, I noticed a lady acting peculiar. I walked over to her and asked what was going on. She said she overheard me and, strangely, her neck pain also went away in the same instant. It seems she saw what I was doing and received the healing as well. Bravo for her receiving it as her own! Be intentional about your walk with Jesus, and you will see these miracles happening in your life!

13
—
IMPARTATION OF GIFTS

The gifts of the Spirit are the best gifts I have ever received!

Impartation means to grant or bestow. Romans 1:11 says, *"For I long to see you, that I may impart unto you some spiritual gift, to the end ye may be established."*

Paul, the writer of Romans, obviously thought that having spiritual gifts helps one to be established. The spiritual gifts he was talking about can be found in 1 Corinthians 12:7-10, which reads, *"But the manifestation of the Spirit is given to every man to profit withal. For to one is given by the Spirit the word of wisdom; to another the word of knowledge by the same Spirit; To another faith by the same Spirit; to another the gifts of healing by the same Spirit; To another the working of miracles; to another prophecy; to another discerning of spirits; to another divers kinds of tongues; to another the interpretation of tongues:"* Furthermore, in 2 Timothy 1:6 Paul says, *"Wherefore I put thee in remembrance that thou stir up the gift of God, which is in thee by the putting on of my hands."* Here the apostle Paul is telling his mentee, Timothy, to use the gift that Paul himself imparted to him, by the laying on of his hands. Another excellent example of this can be found in 1 Timothy 4:14 (but I'll let you look that one up yourself).

I believe that the gifts of the Spirit are available to anyone that would meet the requirements set by the Holy Spirit. I am not saying that you can earn them by works, and I don't claim to know what all these requirements are. I'm merely expressing what 1 Corinthians 12:11 tell us: *"But all these worketh that one and the selfsame Spirit, dividing to every man severally as he will."* As stated in 1 Samuel 16:7, we know that man looks at visible appearances, but God looks at the unseen. It specifically states, *"for man looketh on the outward appearance, but the LORD looketh on the heart."*

The Bible tells us that we can become more Christlike, walking with the same power and authority. I firmly believe that seeking God with a pure and faithful heart is essential to this. What I mean is that it is imperative that you care more about kingdom advancement than your own desires. Trust in God and surrender everything to Him. In return, He will trust in you, exalting you above all the circumstances of life. Due to my faith and trust in God, He entrusted me with the gift of healing. He knew that it wouldn't go unused. He knew that I would step out and practice this gift. Glory to God, by being bold and walking in the power and authority given to us by God Himself, I have seen so many healing miracles over the span of the last five to six years that I can't even count them all. All it took was my obedience to Him. This is my testimony. God does not favor any one person over the other; therefore, He will do the same for you. All you must do is obey Him and completely surrender to Him. Keep in mind that you don't necessarily need the "gift" of healing to see healing miracles.

John 14:13-14 says, *"And whatsoever ye shall ask in my name, that will I do, that the Father may be glorified in the Son. If ye shall ask any thing in my name, I will do it."* **What Jesus is clearly** saying here is that if we ask for something that He knows will glorify the Father, then Jesus will do it for us. Healing people, done in the name of Jesus, definitely qualifies. I was at a local fast food chicken restaurant in the Los Angeles area. I thought I had a word of knowledge about an employee's back being sore, so I asked her, but she replied with a "no." However, she did tell me that she actually had a hurt knee and that she was scheduled to have surgery on it. I further sensed that she had one leg shorter than the other. As with usual practice, I sat her down and in the name of Jesus grew the shorter leg out. All of the pain in her other knee went away as well! She was amazed. I made sure to let her know that this little miracle was Jesus and not I. She went back to work behind the counter, and I could see her talking to her co-workers and looking at me. About five minutes later, after having finished my meal, I walked up to the counter to tell her that I was writing a book on healing. I ask her if she would be willing to email me with her testimony on how this healing miracle had changed her life, as I was hoping to include it in my book. In response, she showed me her arm. I could see goose bumps all over it. Although she never did email me, I could tell that she had experienced an encounter with Jesus that day. I fully believe that she and her co-workers will never be the same.

I was at a conference six years ago at my church in Pasadena, California. Randy Clark was speaking that night. He is a mighty man of God who goes around the world, imparting the gift of healing, and has seen thousands healed in his ministry. He said that he was going to impart the gift of healing to the audience of about 1,000 people. I was near the back of the auditorium with my wife and our friend Lori. Randy told us that all those who received the gift would feel tingling in their hands. With my hands held high, I started to feel a sense of pressure mixed with an electric tingling in my right hand. These sensations began to work their way into my left hand and pointer finger. I had friends at the same conference who were disappointed that they didn't feel anything. I don't know why they didn't receive it, but I believe that God wants us to have it more than we do. We just need to renew our minds to want the will of the Father more than anything else. Needless to say, this encounter changed my life. It gave me the confidence that I needed to walk out and heal the sick. I have imparted this gift to many since then. The gift is not from me or Randy but from God.

To this day, I still feel the electric tingling in my hands when I minister to people and can sense the power leaving my body, going through my hands, and onto the sick. I now impart this gift to others in my classes, and many confirm that they, too, feel tingling or pressure, and some even feel heat in their hands. I recently imparted this gift to my online class, and a student 3,000 miles away felt the tingling in her hands, and she is walking out in many healings now. My online classes are recorded, and if a student misses a class, they can watch it later. A pastor in Arizona watched the class that I imparted the gift of healing three days after the class and felt the tingling go through his hands. The spiritual realm has no time or physical boundaries. I again want to emphasize that although I have the gift of healing, you don't actually need it to see the sick healed. It is like Smith Wigglesworth says, "Just believe," and you, too, will see healing miracles.

If you are really hungry for this confirmation of His power, you can receive it in different ways. A few years back, I was at a Jesus Culture concert where Reinhard Bonnke was speaking. While he was talking, I sensed a nudge from God to extend my hands out. At that moment, I felt a surge of power rush into my hands like I had never felt before. It was exhilarating and almost surreal. During his message, Reinhard said, "Some of you here will be a part of the revival in America." That day I went home blown away by what I had experienced. And that night, I had a dream where thousands of people were being healed. What I experienced earlier that day was so intense that it woke me up every hour or so and I'd feel the surge of power in my hands. That same night, I also dreamt of two men getting into a fight. One killed the other, but as I laid hands on him, he was raised from the dead. I haven't personally seen anyone raised from the dead yet, but it is essential to know that I don't have to see it to actually determine who I am in Christ. We have the same power in us that raised Jesus from the dead, as it states in Romans 8:11.

About five years ago, I was reading a book called *God's Generals*. The book tells stories of some of the healing evangelists from the past. When I was reading the chapter on William Branham, I felt a connection to him. I discovered that he was from Indiana near where I grew up. As I was reading about a visitation from an angel that he had experienced, I came upon a part of the chapter that fascinated me: I read that Branham felt electricity or tingling in his hands when he detected sickness in someone — the exact same thing that I experience. The chapter also said that his hands would become red and puffy, and once the person was healed, his hands would return to their normal state. Upon reading this, something incredible happened. My own hands suddenly turned red and puffy. Electricity started to run through them, and an oil-like substance appeared in the palm of my hands. Glory to God, in that very moment I had received impartation just by reading about Branham!

14
—
HEALING THE SICK

This is the easiest thing that I do — because He has already done it!

There are so many opinions on this subject, and I certainly don't fully understand how it all works. I believe that the only one that has sound theology is Jesus. However, if we remain humble and are open to admit that we don't know it all, the Holy Spirit will teach us all things (see John 14:26). Sometimes He teaches through others, while other times through revelation. As I have stated, I have seen hundreds of healing miracles and will explain to you what has worked for me. It is clear that healing was covered in the atonement. On the cross Jesus provided for our salvation as well as for the healing of our bodies. By reading the Scriptures, we know that God wants all people reconciled to Him and to receive salvation. To receive salvation, one only has to accept Jesus Christ as their Lord and Savior.

Romans 10:8-9 says, *"But what saith it? The word is nigh thee, even in thy mouth, and in thy heart: that is, the word of faith, which we preach; That if thou shalt confess with thy mouth the Lord Jesus, and shalt believe in thine heart that God hath raised him from the dead, thou shalt be saved."* This Scripture clearly states that it takes faith in Jesus to receive salvation. This tells me that even non-believers have faith. If they didn't have any, they couldn't be saved. Isaiah 53:5 says, "*and with his stripes we are healed.*" This Scripture is talking about the stripes of Jesus. Now fast forward to the New Testament, specifically to 1 Peter 2:24, where it says "*by whose stripes ye were healed.*" 1 Peter was written after Jesus died on the cross and is using the past tense by saying the words "*ye were healed.*" We were healed because Jesus already provided for it the day He died on that cross!

Let's take a look at Matthew 8:17: "*Himself took our infirmities, and bare our sicknesses.*" This scripture is quoting what Isaiah had prophesied about Jesus. There are many examples in the Scriptures where Jesus said, "*Your faith has healed you.*" Jesus makes it clear that the level of faith we have is directly correlated to the healing that takes place. When administering healing, I personally approach it believing that they are already healed "by His stripes." Knowing that Jesus has already provided for it makes it easier for us to believe in it. Sometimes, if I feel led, I will quote some of these Scriptures to people to help increase their faith. When healing the sick, just expect it to work and do not let anything take that belief away from you. All you need is to have faith in Jesus and in what the Word of God says you can do. John 14:12 says, "*Verily, verily, I say unto you, He that believeth on me, the works that I do shall he do also; and greater works than these shall he do; because I go unto my Father.*"

Before I get into the exciting things of healing, I want to address a common question that I get asked: Why doesn't everybody get healed? The short answer is I don't know. However, in the Bible we learn that faith is definitely involved in healings, and I will just leave it at that. I have read many books on healing, and some of the explanations I've read that might contribute to people not getting healed are as follows: not being able to forgive others, bitterness, unbelief, or the thought that "God wants me sick to teach me something." The latter one here is difficult for me to accept. It really saddens me that there are people who actually believe this. God loves us, and yes, He does correct us through lessons; however, afflicting us with disease is not of God. I have never met anyone that learned or gained anything from cancer, or any other disease for that matter, other than heartache and pain. I feel that this false belief will prevent their healing. Furthermore, I don't believe that the healing Scriptures that God has given us throughout the Bible are only applicable to "some" people. I believe they are meant for all of His followers.

Let's take a more in-depth look at the matters of the heart, i.e., bitterness and the inability to forgive. I do believe that these can be a hindrance to being healed, to some degree. However, my opinion is that if the individual struggling with such heart matters has a solid belief in Jesus, he or she wouldn't be grappling with these sins in their life. By "strong belief" I mean that the individual has already renewed his or her mind to the extent that they believe what the Word of God says and are able to receive His love and grace. Unbelief is the root cause of the inability to forgive, of bitterness, and of all other sins, i.e., sins that hold you back from receiving the grace of God. It's not that God punishes you because of these sins, but that you don't receive His healing because you don't believe that you can due to your sins. Hebrews 8:12 states that He will no longer remember our sins.

One Sunday at church, while praying for somebody's healing, a random woman interrupted me. She impatiently said she needed healing. I told her she needed to wait until I finished with the person I was with. She lashed out, "Well, Jesus didn't take so long to pray for healing." Operating out of my flesh, I became a little bitter towards her. As I finished with the person I was with, I looked around for the impatient woman with the attitude and noticed that she was on the phone, so I proceeded to pray for the next person in line. After she finished her call, she rudely interrupted me again, so I told her I would be with her in a minute. If I wasn't sure I had bitterness towards her before, I sure did now, and it was apparent that she, too, was bitter to-wards me. But that didn't stop God from healing her. She got her healing, gave me a big hug, and happily went on her way. The lesson I learned that day was that bitterness certainly doesn't stop a person's healing because, in the end, our faith trumps all bitterness.

While reading through my journal one night, I found the following entry from January 25, 2015: "The Holy Spirit revealed to me that when people have anger or 'un-forgiveness' in their heart, God still wants them healed, but they are so stressed that they sometimes can't receive the healing. Their belief is not strong enough to receive healing because of the depressive state they are in and because they are focusing on the problem rather than on Jesus, the healer." After reading this in my jour-nal, I sat down and read my Bible. I read Hebrews 3:12-13, which says, "*Take heed, brethren, lest there be in any of you an evil heart of unbelief, in departing from the living God. But exhort one another daily, while it is called Today; lest any of you be hardened through the deceitfulness of sin.*" Wow! Unbelief comes from an evil heart and leads to the hardening of the heart as well as sin. When we have belief, all things work for us. We can't enter into His rest with unbelief (Hebrews 3:19).

The last hindrance that I mentioned is unbelief. Matthew 13:58 says, "*And he did not many mighty works there because of their unbelief.*" As you can see from this verse, even Jesus could not do many works due to their unbelief. This unbelief took place in Jesus' own hometown. They had unbelief that He was our Savior and thought of Him as just a carpenter. Therefore, I strongly believe that "unbelief" is the act of having heard the Word of God, yet not believing in it. Many Scriptures relate to people being healed due to their own faith. Unbelief is simply believing in the wrong thing. In Mark 10:52 this man believed in the right thing. When a blind man approached Jesus, asking him for his sight back, "*Jesus said unto him, Go thy way; thy faith hath made thee whole. And immediately he received his sight, and followed Jesus in the way.*"

I recently phoned Technical Support, as I needed help with my webpage. During our conversation, I asked the Lord how I could minister to the gentleman helping me. I felt a slight discomfort in my neck, so I asked him to confirm whether or not he was experiencing any pain in that area. Pausing for a few seconds, he replied that he did and went on to explain how his neck pops and cracks every time he moves it. I then asked him if he was a Christian, and he replied "no." I asked if I could pray for his neck, and he said "no." I ignored his "no" as I decided to listen to God and not him, and proceeded to command his neck to be healed in the name of Jesus. He went about helping me with my webpage, and when we finished, I asked him to move his neck around and see how it felt. He did and explained that all the popping and cracking was gone.

Now, I know what you're thinking: How did this guy get healed if he didn't have the faith for it, seeing as how he was a non-believer?" Well, it is simple. To begin, this guy didn't know about needing faith to receive healing. He also didn't know God. Therefore, my faith alone caused the healing miracle to happen. Unlike many Christians, he didn't have unbelief about the fact that Jesus could or would heal him. God gave us His Word (the Bible) and expects us to believe every word in it.

During John G. Lake's ministry in Texas, he put out a statement saying that he would give anyone who didn't get healed $500. However, they would have to attend a month of his teachings on healing before claiming their $500. After two weeks, over half of the students had received healing. Once the month was over, he didn't have to pay anyone $500. The truth will set you free — if you believe the truth!

People can become offended when you suggest to them that they may not have enough faith to be healed. I already wrote about this in the chapter on faith but felt it worth repeating this story. Mark 9:24 says, "*Lord, I believe; help thou mine unbelief.*" This is the story where the disciples couldn't cast the demon out of the man's son. The man asked Jesus to help if He could. Jesus told him, "*If you can believe that all things are possible to those that believe.*" It is possible to have belief and unbelief at the same time. We all have unbelief at different times and situations in our lives. Our unbelief can counterbalance the faith that we do have. Do everything you can to rid yourself and the person you are ministering to of unbelief. But in the end I will take the chance of offending someone to help them work on their unbelief to get them healed. Jesus did this in Matthew 17:20 to explain why the disciples could not cast the demon out of the man's son. So Jesus said to them, "*Because of your unbelief: for verily I say unto you, If ye have faith as a grain of mustard seed, ye shall say unto this mountain, Remove hence to yonder place; and it shall remove; and nothing shall be impossible unto you.*"

In Matthew 17:21 Jesus says that this kind only comes out by fasting and praying. I believe He is talking about how this kind of unbelief comes out by fasting and praying. Focus on Him and trust in Him, and your unbelief will dwindle away.

When I get a word of knowledge for someone, I know that

they are going to be healed because I think, "Why would God give me the word if He wasn't going to heal them?" Jesus went around healing many people without ever asking them whether or not they were oppressed by the devil or harbored any negative emotions, i.e., anger, resentment, grudges, etc. I believe that faith trumps most hindrances of healing. I think some people fail to see many healed because they are looking for all the reasons that may hinder the healing. My suggestion is to not think about any of these things, but instead stand on what the Word of God says about healing.

When you are about to administer healing to someone, you need to first ask the person to briefly explain their problem. For instance, if it is their shoulder that is in pain, ask them to raise their arm up so that you can see how much restriction of movement they have. Then ask them what the pain level is. You'll specifically want them to rate the pain on a scale of 1 to 10, 10 being the highest level of pain. Sometimes they want to go into a long dissertation of what the problem is. Try to stop them, as we don't want them to focus on the negative too much. After praying, monitor the progress by asking them to move about and rate the pain level again. Keep doing this until the pain level drops significantly or disappears altogether. Keep going after it — you will succeed. When I hear something like "stage 3 liver cancer," I will usually reply by saying, "Oh, that's easy for Jesus." I am always trying to let them know how easy it is in hopes that it will take the stress off them. To put them at ease further and remove any resistance, I joke around with them, saying stuff like, "Your job is to receive and not pray. My job is to stand here and look pretty and to let Jesus do the healing. I am not very good at my job, but I assure you that He is." I am confident that they have already prayed for their condition in the past and have not yet received their healing. That is the reason why I ask them not to pray. I don't want any effort on their part other than be-lieving and opening themselves up to receive their healing.

If they have a back problem, I almost always have them sit down and measure their legs to see if one is shorter than the other. Have them put their butt square against the back of a chair and pick up their legs. Make sure they are not angled to one side but perfectly straight. Put the heels together and see if one heel is further out than the other. Don't look at their toes because they can go back and forth. And then just simply command the shorter leg to grow out even with the other leg. It always works. After growing the leg out, I tell them to walk 10 feet over and back, and the pain will be gone. If the pain is not gone, pray over it again and tell it to leave.

If they know why they are experiencing their problem, try to find out specifics. For instance, if it is a vision problem, they may tell you that their cornea is scratched. So you speak specif-ically to the problem and say, "In the name of Jesus, I command the cornea to be repaired right now."

My biggest advice to you is to always be led by the Holy Spirit. Back in 2013, God told me to slow down when praying for people and to listen to Him. This is where I learned this lesson of being led by the Spirit. Your time alone with God will help you learn how to decipher the Holy Spirit's voice. Sometimes while praying for others, I close my eyes so that I can hear from Him better. Some don't recommend closing your eyes because they say that in case he or she has a demonic spirit in them, while you are praying for them, they might try to physically attack you. In response to this, I'm just going to say that I believe the Holy Spirit has our backs.

I was once praying for a lady with rheumatoid arthritis. Her left hand was stiff with pain and had limited movement. As I was commanding the pain to leave and casting out the spirit of arthritis, I sensed that she had pain in her lower back. I, of course, went after this pain by commanding it to leave her. Directly after, I sat her down and ordered the left leg to grow out even with the right, which it did. When I was done praying, the pain in her hand and back were gone, and she now had freedom of movement. She asked me how I knew about her back pain and about her shorter leg. She was surprised because she had never mentioned any of those things to me. This is when you want to tell them that Jesus loves them so much that He let you know about their pain to get rid of it for them.

You see, this sort of stuff can happen to you as well. You might begin to pray for someone's healing, and in the middle of it, God can give you a word of knowledge about something else that they need prayer for. Live a life focused on Him, and over time you'll look back in amazement at how much you, too, have grown in this area of your relationship with Jesus. I know that this can be difficult for some of you. Don't concentrate on your anointing or lack thereof, but rather on His presence. Do your best in getting those that you are praying for to be aware of His presence. Keep pressing in to be able to release His power and authority in healing and in words of knowledge, and ask the Holy Spirit for help. Just remember that He wants you to walk in His fullness even more than you do. If I can do it, anyone can.

Whether you know it or not, you have Christ in you. Galatians 2:20 confirms this: "*I am crucified with Christ: nevertheless I live; yet not I, but Christ liveth in me: and the life which I now live in the flesh I live by the faith of the Son of God, who loved me, and gave himself for me.*" In Jesus there is a lot of peace. You can release this peace to others through prayer. A phrase you can use when you first begin your prayer for someone is "I release peace into you, more and more peace." Anytime I've ever done this, the individual I'm praying for always reports feeling an immense amount of peace in their body. Their stress and anxiety level, rigid resistance, doubt, embarrassment — anything that is negative dissipates as peace washes over them. I believe that once this happens, they are better able to receive their healing.

I sometimes like to increase the person's faith before I pray for his or her healing. I do this by telling them a testimony of healing that I have experienced. I then ask them if they believe that Jesus wants to heal them. In the instance they don't, I ask them, "Why wouldn't He want to heal you?" I assure them that Jesus does want to heal them and that they are made righteous through Jesus Christ. I tell them that nothing they have ever done disqualifies them from the healing that they are about to experience. Sometimes I tell people not to worry about their faith because I have enough faith for the both of us. I assure them that they are going to be healed right now — not tomorrow — but right now.

Once, a lady at church came up to me with a lot of pain in her back and could only walk with a walker. She had been in this condition for 20 years. I sat her down and grew her leg out, but she still had pain, which went down from a 7 out of 10 to about 5. When I see some improvement, I will sometimes have them speak to the pain. I want to show them that they have the same Jesus in them that I have. I say that my Jesus is no bigger than theirs. She started by asking God to remove anything that she had done in the past that would stop this healing, so I stopped her and said that nothing that she had done would stop her from being healed. So I took back over and commanded the pain to leave. After doing this a few times, for the first time in 20 years she was walking pain-free without the walker! Her friend was amazed and said she couldn't do that before, as she was tearing up.

Because the Holy Spirit isn't restricted to any boundaries, I get to see a lot of healings over the phone. While driving to work one day, I called a guy that a friend referred me to. I didn't know anything about this guy except that he had stomach problems. He was released from the hospital a few weeks prior because they couldn't figure out what was the matter with him. He was now at home, flat on his back, unable to eat and very weak. I asked him if he knew that he had the same power in him that raised Jesus from the dead. He said he didn't, but I could tell by his voice that he believed me. I told him, "Yes, look it up: Romans 8:9 and Ephesians 1:19-20." At this point I was being led by the Spirit and speaking with confidence and authority. I don't remember exactly what I said, but when I got done, he was excited. He said, "The first time you cast it out, I could feel rumbling in my stomach, and the second time you did, I felt it again, and all the pain went away." He was able to eat twice that day and is doing well now. There is no end to what we can accomplish; we can do what hospitals can't do. Always approach people with confidence — because you, too, have the same power in you that raised Jesus from the dead.

One of the biggest mistakes I notice that people make is when they "ask" God for the healing. Don't "ask" God, but rather "command" the healing "in the name of Jesus Christ." An example of this would be if you say, "In the name of Jesus Christ, I command the pain to leave you right now." Another way of doing it would be to say, "In the name of Jesus Christ, I command the eyes to open." In other words, command the negative to go away, and speak life into it. Proverbs 18:21 says, "*Death and life are in the power of the tongue: and they that love it shall eat the fruit thereof.*" In Mark 11:23 Jesus says, "*For verily I say unto you, That whosoever shall say unto this mountain, Be thou removed, and be thou cast into the sea; and shall not doubt in his heart, but shall believe that those things which he saith shall come to pass; he shall have whatsoever he saith."* **Notice that Jesus says to speak to the mountain.**

A young lady approached me on the ministry team, walking with a cane and in apparent pain. The doctor told her that she needed surgery because the muscles and tendons attached to her patella were not strong enough. I had the lady I was mentoring grow her leg out, but that didn't solve the problem. So I commanded the ligaments, tendons, and muscles to strengthen around her patella. She was instantly healed and started running and jumping! She had endured this problem for two and a half years and had thought about suicide. She is so happy not to have to take all the daily pain pills anymore, and I now see her at church up front dancing. There are many people out there who are not being healed because there are not enough of us willing to be responsible for the power that Jesus empowered us with and trusted us to feed His sheep.

I once ordered a lady's kidneys to function, and she could feel them reposition in her body. I then spoke to her liver, and she could feel it responding. When we believe, we receive. Knowing that Jesus has given you the authority and the power to do the works that He did and more magnificent works than those, we should gain a certain level of confidence to speak to a problem with power and conviction while believing it will be healed and made whole.

If you don't see results after commanding it to happen, go after it again. Find out if the pain level went down at all. Even if it went down a little, praise God for what He just did. Believe in what Jesus did on the cross and remember that the healing is already done. Jesus said it is finished. He didn't say, "I have a few more things to do and will get back to you soon." If the person you are praying for has seen some improvement, ask them to speak to the problem themselves as I stated earlier. Sometimes when they are actually able to detect the results of their own prayer, it gives them the confidence that they can do it again later in case the pain were to come back. I tell them that they have the same Jesus in them that I do and that my Jesus isn't any bigger than theirs.

After they are healed, it is essential to let them know how to hold onto their healing. I will usually quote John 10:10: "*The thief cometh not, but for to steal, and to kill, and to destroy: I am come that they might have life, and that they might have it more abundantly.*" Let them know that Satan will try to steal their healing, but that they, too, have the same power that raised Jesus from the dead. They should command any symptom that returns to leave in the name of Jesus Christ. I will usually tell them my testimony of when I was first healed at Bethel Church in Redding, about eight years ago, from a "frozen shoulder." As you may recall from my testimony, I tell them that I couldn't raise my arm any higher than about 30 degrees, but after they prayed over me, I could raise it all the way up with almost no pain. And to test my healing, on the way home I put my arm out to the side and could raise it straight out in front of the passenger chair at a 90-degree angle. This was amazing to me because I wasn't able to do that before. I then explain to them how I proceeded to put my arm behind the passenger seat and immediately felt pain shoot into my shoulder. I then go on to tell them how I could clearly hear Satan say to me, "Darrell, you stupid idiot. You didn't get healed." I then remembered what they said to me at Bethel after I received my healing. I followed their advice and commanded the pain to go away in the name of Jesus, and it promptly left me. I end my testimony by telling them that when we speak with belief and authority, nothing can stop the power of God.

Definitively this healing was a turning point in my life. I had only been a Christian for about three years then, still having doubts about God's existence and not entirely sure how eternity worked. This confusion caused me to doubt my belief in God. After this healing, however, everything changed. Jesus became real to me. That is why I am so passionate about healing. I know it changes people's lives. I have seen so many people cry and be overcome with emotion when they experience the power of God going through their body, healing them. These individuals will never be the same, and, in turn, they can now be a more excellent witness for the kingdom.

Proverbs 4:20-22 says, "*My son, attend to my words; incline thine ear unto my sayings. Let them not depart from thine eyes; keep them in the midst of thine heart. For they are life unto those that find them, and health to all their flesh.*"

Most people haven't renewed their minds enough to have the revelation that God has already provided for their healing. They don't have pure faith that their healing is the direct result of what the Word of God says. The more you can educate them on this topic, the better chance they will have to hold onto their healing.

I usually ask God for words of knowledge when I go to public places or hang out in the lobby before Sunday church service. God can speak words of knowledge to us via different methods. He might show you a vision of a person's body part, or give you slight pain or discomfort in a certain area of your body, or you might just know where the person's body is aching. In some instances God might make the person's pain or discomfort known to you without you actually feeling anything. When He does any of these things, He'll usually "highlight" the person to you. By "highlight" I mean that He will direct your attention towards the individual that He wants you to minister to. It's almost like God is shining a spotlight on them.

The key is to ask God for these words with faith so that He will give them to you. Remember always that He does not favor any one person over the other. Therefore, anybody can walk in the gift of the word of knowledge. This is a powerful tool because the person you approach with a word of knowledge is usually shocked and impressed that God used you to care about their pain or situation. You will see many healed this way. One thing I know for sure: This ministry is a lot of fun, so relax, believe in what the Word of God says, and enjoy the ride.

So remember to keep it simple. Whatever the problem they may have, just speak to it in the name of Jesus, and it will be done.

I leave you now with my last words. BELIEVE in all that is written in God's Word, and, in turn, you will see your faith soar higher than you have ever imagined. A life transformed demonstrates our faith through our works. So step out. Remember: You have to care more about kingdom advancement than what people are going to think about you.

"My soul, wait thou only upon God; for my expectation is from him. He only is my rock and my salvation: he is my defence; I shall not be moved. In God is my salvation and my glory: the rock of my strength, and my refuge, is in God."

Psalm 62:5-7

I am currently teaching online healing/ impartation classes attended by people all over the country.

To learn more, please visit my webpage:

WWW.GODDEPENDENCE.ORG

If you have any questions about healing or my classes, you can email me directly:

DARRELL@GODDEPENDENCE.ORG

Have fun and change the world — you can do this!